What My Father Never Taught Me About Being A Real Man

Lessons to Teach Every Man and Their Sons

Shawn James

How to Use this Book

This book is simply one to be used for young men and grown men as the coaching and learning tool for development. I created this to be a guide for discussions among boys' and men's organizations. Suggested use can be as follows:

1. To use as a mentoring tool for one on one coaching.
2. To use as a coaching tool for a small group of boys or men.
3. To use in church organizations to discuss certain issues.
4. To use as a reading assignment and discussion.
5. To use for single mothers who need to teach their sons lessons.
6. To use for fathers who want to teach their sons lessons.
7. As a gift from girlfriends and spouses to polish up on men's issues.
8. As a book for teaching for our incarcerated brothers.

The list can go on but these are just a few examples of how I want to help develop our men to reach higher levels of greatness. I pray and encourage that everyone who reads these words are enlightened and become better men.

At the end of this book I would enjoy getting your reviews on how you enjoyed the book. Please send all reviews and comments to:

realmanbookcomments@gmail.com

Thank you for reading this book.

Shawn James

TABLE OF CONTENTS

ACKNOWLEDGMENTS

I want to give special thanks to my father Henry C. James Jr. for being a father to me. I want to thank my mother Ann Jackson for being the greatest mother and teaching me right from wrong, and thinking for myself.

Special thanks go to my daughter Brianna who is the light of my life, and my sister Heather--they are the reasons I wrote this book to always be a real man for them and to help the younger generation of boys become real men for them to depend on.

To Tina, thank you for your ongoing support and encouragement.

To Keisha Rivers Shorty, thank you for your guidance, encouragement, editing assistance, and helping me to embark on this journey of teaching, sharing and mentoring.

To my Prince Hall Masonic Lodge, Plymouth Rock #86 for being the brothers that I needed to help mold me into being a better man after my father passed.

I also thank all my uncles, cousins, teachers, mentors, and friends that all helped to mold me and shape me as a man through the years. It's because of all of you that have inspired me to give back.

Thank you ---- Shawn.

DEDICATION

This book is dedicated to those who encouraged me, who supported me, who challenged me, who prayed for me, and to those who hated against me.

This is also dedicated to my all my brothers across the globe. This is for the sons, the fathers, the brothers, the nephews, the uncles, and grandfathers. This is also for those who are lost and those that wish to be found.

This is my legacy and my gift that I present to you. I pray that every man receive something of quality and content, and pass it on to another male.

I humbly thank you.

INTRODUCTION

"Look son, stop being a punk! "

"If you don't go back and beat that bully up, then I will go and cut your ass right here where you stand!"

Ha-ha. Now that is a line that my friend's dad told him when he was thirteen about the neighborhood bully (who, by the way, was fourteen years old) when they were facing off and about to fight in the front yard. His dad told him to basically "grow some balls" and go fight this bully, or else that bully would terrorize him for the rest of his time in school.

Have you ever heard that?

How about this one?

"Boy, stop being a wuss and go talk to that pretty girl!"

This is what's being shouted at you, and all the while you may be rooted to the spot, saying to yourself, "But, I don't know what to say".

Okay, so maybe that wasn't you. Maybe it's something else, like: 'make sure you give a firm and strong handshake when you shake someone's hand' or 'look me in the eyes when I'm talking to you son' or 'stand up straight and speak up'.

No matter what was told to you back then, I still find that a lot of young men--and even grown men for that matter--are still missing the mark time and time again.

First, a word of warning.

If you're looking for political-correctness about this issue, then this isn't the book for you. But if you want real talk—straight, in-your-face, no-holds-barred talk—then this is EXACTLY the book for you. This is a conversation. It's me sitting down talking to you—man to man. This book is meant for boys who aspire to be men and for men who desire to lead with conviction and love.

Some of the messages in this book are stated in a way that is real, raw and in-your-face. It's not done to offend, although some may take offense. It is meant to teach--and to reach--those who need it. If that is you or someone you know, then great. If this isn't for you, then pass it along to someone else.

I wrote this book to get past the fluff and filler and deal with the truth—bottom-line.

And the stinking truth of the matter is that each and every day here in America the "real men"—those with attitude, strength, class, swagger, and leadership abilities---are slowly being diminished and diluted in this metro-sexual bullcrap!

This pains me to see. So, I decided to write a book to address these cultural problems within our male species and give some real concrete advice and tools for our young men--and grown men--to use immediately.

First of all, I want you to understand that MAN is the greatest and strongest creature alive on the planet, and we have a power that is unlike any other that is only next to GOD himself.

Wow! Powerful stuff I say.

Hell yeah it is!

Come on men, do you know that we create life like Adam, and that Eve was taken from Adam's rib?

Do you understand that next to GOD, men are created in HIS image?

The problem that I am seeing and witnessing every day is how grown men are acting more and more like whining females (no offense, ladies). Men are now throwing temper tantrums, and crying after women like they are little girls. I'm just not understanding--where is our testosterone going to men?

I keep hearing that the number of dads in the home raising our sons is declining dramatically. I keep hearing that our sons are coming out of the closet more because they are imitating their mothers. I keep hearing about more boys and men who are hitting on women, but are not man enough to fight another man that disrespects their women. I keep hearing more and more men that stop becoming providers and are living in the woman's home, or the woman is taking care of the man and that it's okay because times are changing.

BULLCRAP!!!!

Young men and seasoned men this MUST STOP!!

I am here to tell you through this book that it is totally unacceptable to continue for our men to behave and operate in this manner.

The following pages of this book will be the honest and solid truth and contain information that you need to conduct yourself as a young man and as a grown man.

The information enclosed in these pages make up the tools

needed to become the man that GOD intended for you to be. The man that your girlfriend, your wife, your mother, your sister, your community, and your family intended for you to be.

I'm telling you men these are not optional things---these are MANDATORY things that must be followed and acknowledged as the building blocks necessary to successfully be a man in today's world and to secure our men's future.

With that being said, all that I ask--my young men and grown men--is that you honestly read this book one time from cover to cover; implement the things that you learn and then pass this book on to another man so that he may learn also.

If you do that, then we can create an army of strong men with the pride, integrity, strength, high self-esteem, and respect that all men deserve--and are destined--to have.

Is this for me?

This book is for all men, all creeds, all colors, and all races. These words are for all boys, teenagers, young men, and seasoned men.

If you are not looked up to as a man, then most likely it is because you are not acting like one. If you are not being respected or revered as a strong man, then I assure you it is because you are not acting like one.

This is the first sign that you do not have all the pieces of the puzzle. If you are not being a full man, then how the hell can you teach a young boy to be a full man?

I'm not going to sugar coat anything my fellow brothers. If I do, then you won't get it and you cannot then respect my words.

This is the time to get off your ass and really look deep inside yourself and find out why those around you are not calling you a "Real Man".

You cannot be fake here.

You cannot front and lie, then be a scared little boy hiding in your room when no one is looking.

It's time to address the issues of abuse, molestation, weakness, infidelity, bullying, insecurities, shyness, seclusion, anger, depression, lying, etc.

Please understand my brothers--I call you all brothers because we all are brothers in this struggle for manhood--You are not alone. Millions of boys and men around the world are struggling to find their way down this path of manhood.

Again, I assure you, some of you have been on this journey for a few years; some are just beginning the journey; whereas others have been searching for the truth and the answers their whole lives.

It's okay. God had us meet up together here in this book with these words just for you, so we can all get on the right path to get our brotherhood back in order.

I thank you all for purchasing this book, borrowing this book, or just picking up this book to read. My message is clear, BECOME BETTER MEN, THEN TEACH THE NEXT MAN!

Let's get started!

1ST LESSON: BEING A MAN

What does being a man mean?

So, let's start this conversation my brothers.

Everyone out here is coming up with their thoughts and ideas of what today's man should be. Is he tough; is he a bad-ass; is he the jock, the bully, or the guy with the money and all the women?

The first lesson here is to learn *just to be who you are.* You can be the funny guy, the smart guy, the nerd, the smart-ass, the jock, the money maker—but no matter who you are, let's start building confidence that you are who God made you to be--simple as that.

A man is a person who can learn what his strengths and weaknesses are, and can learn to work with those strengths, and enhance his weaknesses.

A man **is** strong. He is strong with his mind, and can be strong with his body. A man is stronger than the woman by body composition, but he is destined to be strong in his spirit.

"What the heck are you talking about Shawn?"

I'm saying that a man has the desire to be focused and conquer, and succeed in acquiring goals. We do this by thinking strategically and methodically. We see this by putting up pictures, playing our favorite songs with meanings in them, by practicing our favorite sports until we are perfect, or working those long tiring hours to hustle and get what we need.

As men we can and will do dumb stuff to accomplish our goals. We may follow the girl we like, and watch her for hours, days, or even weeks until we figure out how we can approach her and make her our girlfriend or even our wife. This is okay fellas, this is how we are designed as conquerors.

We may work those long hours trying to get that money for our car, support our families, or buy that dream home we see in the magazine so we can be somebody. This is who we are men, we do things to conquer our goals--and it is okay that we operate this way. So being a man is listening to that hungry, determined voice inside us saying we got to get whatever it is we want and desire. So being a man is being a conqueror!

We are all conquerors men!

But I Never Had A Dad!

Okay, my brothers. This is going to be the hard section here but we are going to get through it together.

This is for all you thugs, boys and men with tempers, the men who are "hoe-ing around", the abusers, the alcoholics, the players, the immature men (you know exactly who you are). I understand and millions of men around the world--yes I said millions--we all can and will understand that some of us experienced the missing link of not having a father around, or of never knowing our dads. This is the unfortunate stuff that God makes us deal with. So, let's deal with it right here and right now!

YOU ARE A GOOD GUY OR MAN EVEN THOUGH YOUR DAD WAS NOT THERE!

Who the hell is that guy who made us or birthed us?

Do I look like him, do I act like him?

Our mothers say we may be just like him, or she never talks about him. What the heck is that about? Brothers, it may be about her being ashamed to talk about him. It may be that she had laid down with a loser, or he just left her because the pressure of having a child was too much for him to handle.

What I have learned is that this has been a cycle men have learned from their dads when it comes to dealing with pressure and them not being man enough to commit to their choices.

I intentionally said "choices" in the last sentence because you are NEVER A MISTAKE.

God has made you for a purpose as a soldier and a conqueror and believe me HE has a very important mission for every man on this planet.

Now, let's understand that it would be nice, and perhaps very helpful to have had a father or dad to be in our lives; but sometimes, my brothers, a lot of your dads were not worth anything to begin with to even be worthy to be considered or called your dad.

Sorry, this is just some real talk for you.

What I want you to know is that sometimes you will have to stand on your own and figure things out. This is why I wrote this book for you, to help you figure out your path and find your way. I am here, with hundreds and thousands of other men, to help you become the man that you are supposed to be and are intended to be in your life.

Not having a dad does not mean that you are any less of a man. What it does mean is that you will have to just focus and work a bit harder to be a great man.

You are and can be a GREAT man.

This is merely a decision that you have to make that without your father you will become a great man. I am whole heartedly dedicated as "**my brother's keeper**", to make sure that with this book, you will have the tools to become a great man.

I need you--and the World needs you--to be a Great Man.

Men Are Built On Respect

You can be a great fighter.

You can be a great debater.

You can be a bodybuilder who looks bigger and stronger than everyone in the gym.

But without "RESPECT", you have _nothing_ my brothers.

Let's discuss this in depth.

Respect is the backbone of all men.

We tote guns around for respect.

We drive nice expensive cars and wear nice clothes to gain respect.

We date and marry beautiful women and become players sexing numerous women to gain and hold on to respect.

There are even men that kill for respect.

Again, I am just being honest and real about the world of men.

We are strong and potentially violent animals deep, deep inside our souls that attempt to stay civil with each other just for the need and fulfillment of our individual respect.

When boys and men wrestle, fight, or tease each other with verbal jabs it is because we are preserving our respect. Respect is our inner being, part of our soul, it's almost the reason for living, and can even be the downfall to our death. We need respect, and we need those around us to respect us as growing men.

Brothers, here is the lesson I need you to know and understand. Simply by carrying yourself as a strong and confident man who can be humble when necessary, this will help you to gain the greatest respect from others. Telling the truth to others--even when it hurts those closest to you--gains respect. Telling your lady that you want another woman is hurtful, but damn, you cannot do anything but respect that man. Telling another man that he is acting out of order, irresponsible, or stupid is risky but you gain great respect that way from other men. Standing up for something that you know is wrong and making it right gains great respect. Fighting for justice in your neighborhood or on your job when you see things are wrong gains you great respect. You see, without respect no one will follow you or even want to associate with you. What boy or man wants to associate themselves with someone who no one else respects?

Just think about that for a minute.

Who wants to follow a punk, a loser, a liar? Only another punk, another loser, or another liar. Men, stop giving away your respect to others who do not and will not respect you. As a man you must earn and honor your individual respect. I promise you nobody will respect you if you will not learn to respect yourself, and if you cannot earn the respect of others you will get nowhere in this life. Live every day to earn and gain people's respect through your honesty and your good actions.

Real Men Have Honor And Integrity

Every young boy thought of being a policeman, firefighter, a soldier, football player, businessman, etc. when he grew up. But in every profession of whatever it is we thought we wanted to grow up and be, there was a rule that everyone that joined the ranks had to have Honor and Integrity.

What exactly is this and what does it mean to men?

It means that in the old days someone's handshake meant "I respect and honor you" and your handshake was taken to mean that your "word" was good and that it's binding. If I shake your hand then your word as a man is greatly respected.

Integrity means that out of that respect for your handshake and what that symbolizes, you should keep your word. Integrity is saying what you mean, and meaning what you say to be true and honest.

But somewhere in this past half century men's words are becoming CRAP!

For many men their word doesn't mean anything. They offer their word or their hand in honor, but then don't follow through on what they said they'd do. That means that their word is worth nothing at all. It's bogus, it's full of crap, it ultimately means you cannot and will not be trusted among other men. Personally, I cannot respect any man, or person for that matter, that has no honor or integrity. Why should I? If I give them my respect when they don't deserve it then *my* word is CRAP! As a grown man I refuse to have any of my words mean crap.

Brothers we need to show each other honor and integrity at all times. There are some honor and integrity rules that as a real man you must keep. Honor another man's home. Don't disrespect their home with bad language and your nasty appearance.

Have honor when you approach another man and correct him on something. Keep it real and honest. Don't lie or make up stuff which is not true and be man enough to tell the entire truth. If you said it then own up to it! Own your own words. Integrity means that you stand by your words whether they are good ones or bad ones. The reason men have such a problem earning each other's respect is because they flip flop their words so much. This is not the type of man you want to be EVER! Our country fights to be honored by other countries this is why so many people of different nationalities come here to America because our principles are built on honor and integrity.

Years and years have gone by where gangs of young men continue to kill each other every day. Do you know why so many of our young men between the ages of 17 to 27 are dying daily? The answer is because they are looking for respect and they all have a lack of honor and integrity among the ranks. All you gang members out there are crazy killing each other off. As I said we will either live for respect or we will die trying to get respect and honor.

There is absolutely no respect in killing a brother! No matter if he is white, black, brown or other.

This very reason is why our sons will have no respect, honor, or integrity in their lives because this batch of today's men are so lost. We kill our brothers because they walked on the wrong side of the street, or in the wrong neighborhood, or because they were wearing the wrong colors. The lack of honor and integrity is that our young brothers don't even fight fairly. They need a gang of guys to fight one man. They use a gun when they should be man enough to use their hands.

All these young men are lost and are just boys. It's a shame, but here is where it can start to learn what honor and integrity can do for you. If you learn its value my brothers then you will gain all the respect in the world. Honor is saying as a man that I am here to fight for sensible and righteous things, not stupid and dumb things. Integrity is the power to be honest and say this crap is dumb and stupid and I will not stand for this. Brothers you must have honor and integrity or else we will never be true and real men.

Men Are Mature And Responsible

Okay fellas, here is where the rubber meets the road. In other words, here is some real talk on maturity first.

Maturity is the ability to be a grown man even when it's not easy, convenient, or if you like it.

Maturity is growing up.

You know when you guys make sarcastic jokes, or pick fights with your friends, or horseplay around? These things are not mature. Now having fun with your guy friends like that may be okay sometimes, but not all the time. Being that way with a woman you are dating or serious about definitely is not cool at all. Real men must be and appear to be mature. Playing around all the time is not cool or desirable. The problem is that a lot of young men out here do not know how to be mature.

The only way to be mature is to change your circle of friends and associates to those guys or men that are mature. To a lot of you out there you think this means you are giving up the fun. This is not the case, it just means that now you will grow up and find fun in other ways that are necessary for you to succeed and be respected. When you act and are mature then people--especially other men--can trust you and respect you. When you are mature then you can make good decisions and then other people will follow you.

So boys and men out here grow the hell up now!

Now here is a big, big topic we definitely need to talk about brother--it's responsibility. Being responsible gentlemen is the biggest and most important part of being a true and real man. This ties into your word, your bond, your honor, and your integrity and respect. If you are not responsible then you cannot be a real leader. If you cannot be responsible in your life then you will not and cannot be respected.

Being responsible means several different things. It could be doing your homework or doing your housework. It could be completing something that you committed to and said that you were going to do. It could be taking care of your personal business, or taking care of your family or something in your personal relationships. If you cannot be responsible, then you cannot ever be considered a real and true man--point blank.

Let's focus for a minute on my grown men out here that are making these babies and not taking care of them and being responsible. **Men, by not taking care of your children you are messing them up for the future**. I cannot say this any other way. They will grow up not respecting who dad is; they will not fear and respect their dad for the simple reason that he is not there and he is not providing.

Remember you were not being responsible in the beginning when you slept with the girl or women you had sex with, and now you are compounding your mistakes by walking out on the child or children. Through your actions, they will not understand what a true man is or should be—they will not grow up understanding that a true man should behave with honor, respect, and integrity. Yes, I said it. I'm getting on everybody here.

If you are a man between the ages of 17 to 57—you need to understand that we brothers are responsible for our girls and boys that we created. That means our actions and lack of responsibility affect who they become.

Because you are not responsible to them when they are children, our sons will grow up to be thugs, robbers, and even killers. Our little girls will become "hoes", abused, violated, and disrespected.

You see, men, you are the leader in all places. Men set the tone for the world, our countries, and our homes. I told you earlier Eve was taken from man's rib. This means you control all the circumstances that our kids are going through, and those that our women have to endure.

Listen to me when I say men that you must be responsible in everything that you do and say. You cannot be a leader in anyone's home if you cannot be responsible in your own. So, for all of my brothers across the world--it's time to now start to be mature and responsible and start seeing your children, your seeds. It's time to work harder and provide for your one child or fifteen children.

If you are going to be responsible then you may need to get 2 or 3 jobs. It may be time to start your business. It is time to be involved with all your children, yes, even if it means your current girlfriend or spouse gets mad or threatens to leave. If she is a good woman then she will encourage you to be responsible to your children and not leave them out in the cold letting another man teach them their ways and not yours.

Do you really want your child to call another man daddy? If so then you are not responsible. Do you want another man fixing your mistakes and taking care of your responsibilities? If so, then you cannot be respected by any other man--or anyone else for that fact.

It's time to step up my brothers and begin being mature and responsible. It's also time for us as brothers to hold each other accountable to make sure we are being responsible in our relationships, our homes, our businesses, and with our children whether they are with us or not.

Men Are DESTINED To Lead

Since the beginning of time men have been created to lead in the world. Each of you has the ability to be a leader. It is built inside of your DNA. Men were made to have the strength to lead. We were given strong voices--whether light or deep, it does not matter-- we are made to use our voices to lead.

As boys we want to be competitive and this is your leadership abilities growing and developing. When we play sports or just play we have the need to be a leader, the captain, the chief, the general. It is a driving force in all males to want to lead. When we are teenagers and we develop attitude, and start talking back to our parents, it is because our leadership skills are coming out stronger and stronger.

For all of you men trying to understand why we have such strong personalities or we sometimes can be confrontational with people, it is because of our growing need and desire to be leaders.

That's it my brothers.

We are bred and made to be strong leaders.

I need you to really take time out and understand that everything that you do--the trials and the errors--are just the grooming and development that you are going through to become a leader.

Having a relationship and dating is grooming you to become a leader of your household. If you cannot be a leader in your relationships then you will soon realize that someone else has to be a leader to get things done. If you, as the man do not lead and the woman leads, then this certainly will be a big problem.

A girl or woman should not tell you how to be a man. She can help guide you but should not be telling you. As a man, we are expected to step up in situations and take charge. Failure to take charge in situations will immediately cause you to lose respect in other people's eyes. As a man you cannot lose people's respect. A man should always be in a constant development of his leadership skills and in the process of gaining people's respect.

This is why you must have maturity, be responsible, have honor and integrity, and tell the truth--even if it hurts. Leaders do strong things all the time. Leaders grow to be strong in their character. Are you strong in your character?

Here is the thing. If you do not feel that you are being a leader, then this is the time to find out how to be one and start taking on leadership positions. If you just like being in the background and letting other people do things for you that you know you should be doing, then you are not going to be the man that you need to be.

If you are scared, timid, and too shy to step up and take charge of a situation, then you are also not going to be the man that you need to be. If you make excuses as to why you don't want to lead then you cannot be a man. If you whine and complain about taking responsibility for things, then you most certainly cannot be a man.

Remember my brothers are you DESTINED to lead.

Each and every one of us was born to be a leader in some capacity in our lives.

So I know you're asking, "Shawn, how do I become a leader?". First, if you are a young man, then you need to volunteer and become a part of a team. This can be in sports, debate club, Kiwanis club--basically anything other than a GANG!

Gangs are poor and pathetic excuses for a team. These are groups of weak men that thrive on destroying other men. Gangs do not have loyalty, honor, and definitely not respect. If they did then boys and men would not die for what amounts to nothing, instead they would be known to be great for something--and let's face it, no gang is thought of as being "great" at violence and criminal acts.

If you lead a team to victory then this is honorable. What we miss gentlemen is that if you are doing or leading others into criminal activities you are only setting yourself up to be locked up in a cage.

You cannot gain respect or honor inside of a cage. Weak men and weak followers end up in cages. Free men are leaders, and strong respectable men are free. They are free to conquer the challenges of the world and influence people by the hundreds, thousands, and millions. Men lead winning teams, men lead states and countries. Men run for presidency. You see great leaders of the world started out as an ordinary man just like you and I.

So, the best way to become a great leader is to follow a great leader. You must study about great leaders good ones and not so good ones. Then you must surround yourself with strong men that are honorable, good, loyal, respectable, and responsible. Then you must get out there and just "Do It"! Just lead something, somewhere, anywhere you can be a leader then lead. Be a leader in school, at your job, at church, in an organization, in your neighborhood with other young men. Remember there are tons of books, movies, and, mentors that are out here that can show you how to become a good leader but you must not be scared to go out and find out where they are.

The world needs you to be a leader. We need the next team captain, the next coach, the next House representative, the next Senator, even the next President. What we do not need is the next bully, the next gang leader, the next criminal, the next embezzler. We need **men**--not crooks and criminals. Brothers we need you out here being an example of what is right and good. Make a decision to be the good strong leader that God intended each and every man to be.

Men Are Protectors

I grew up believing that men protected their home and their families. Men did not let other men disrespect their mothers, sisters, girlfriends, or wives. Protecting what you were a leader of, meant protecting your respect. If someone disrespected your family or someone you are in a relationship with, then they threatened and disrespected you.

The problem is that too many of us men have lost our respect for ourselves--therefore, in turn, we let others disrespect us by threatening what is ours.

To protect means that your property, your home, your family, and your relationships must have some meaning to you. If they have meaning to you then you should and will protect those things by all reasonable means necessary.

Men, this is exactly what women want from us.

They want to know first, that you care and that they have meaning to you. Your family and your children want to know you care and that they mean something to you. Next, women want to know that you are willing to protect them from harm and disrespect. This doesn't mean men that you get crazily jealous. Being jealous does not mean you are protective. It means you are immature, insecure, and stupid. This is exactly what it means. Do not be caught up in jealousy. Jealousy makes men weak and stupid. You cannot afford to be perceived as weak or stupid.

Now, let's talk a little bit more about being a protector. This does not mean that you as a man need to go out starting a fight because someone talked about your momma.

What this actually means is that you learn to use your head and think. Think about what you need to protect and how. Words are not a reason to get beat up, but someone who puts their hands on you or a loved one may be a reason to get in protection mode.

As men we are physical, this is why we love MMA fighting, football, wrestling, martial arts, and movies and games where things blow up. We understand that being physical means we can be protective.

So here are some rules on being a protector.

1. Only fight when you or someone is threatened.

2. Use your hands before you use a weapon.

3. Only use a weapon when absolutely necessary.

4. When protecting something or someone always think about the serious consequences.

You must be willing to accept responsibility for your protective efforts. But, as a man, make sure you are and feel justified for the means. In other words, stand by your actions.

It's very important that as leaders and men that we are protectors in the world. Providing a feeling of safety is something that men are designed to do for our women, our children, and the weak that cannot protect themselves.

So my fellow brother protectors, be strong and know your role and responsibility to protect our property, our homes, our families and loved ones. Also protect the weak and disabled. This is part of being a man.

Real Men Are Providers

Now, I know that with the present state of our economy this is a sensitive issue for many of us men. I do not blame you for being sensitive. But, we also must speak on this issue because for many of you it has not been taught or explained as to what a provider is and why we as men must be adequate providers. So here we go.

As I stated earlier, men are leaders in the home and outside the home. To be a leader you must work at being a leader in the area of finances.

Now, you may wonder, what if your mate makes more money than you? The dilemma this poses can certainly be understandable. In that instance, the case may be that your mate may want you to look at different avenues to carry part of the load.

Men please understand this point. If there is nothing else that I can emphasize to you—it is this. *Men must work to carry a majority of the load.*

As men we must work harder at providing either by getting an additional job; changing to a better paying job, or starting a business to supplement income while working a full-time job.

Men, a main reason why we are losing respect in our homes and losing our leadership roles is because if you cannot contribute and carry a majority of the financial load then you cannot be respected fully as the "head of household". This is what is expected from a leader in the home.

Please do not get discouraged here. I am not beating you down, but please note that women want SECURITY. This is what security entails--taking care of the finances. Maybe you don't take care of all of the bills, but you need to account for a majority of them, which means more than 50%.

My brothers, you have to understand that men have been providers since the time cavemen walked the earth, and it will always be the role that we must take on. If you are not an adequate provider then you need to take a look at yourself.

One of the reasons our women are constantly at odds with us within the home could be because we are not truly in a satisfactory provider role. Just to show your mate that you are willing to do anything to provide will reap rewards in many ways, plus it will instill in your children that you will do anything legally possible not to take a handout.

Men, if you are relying on women to take care of you and pay your bills this is not what real men do. If you are living off of family members and friends instead of paying your own way, this is pathetic and this is not what real men do. If you are borrowing money and not repaying your debt, this is terrible and is the opposite of having honor and integrity. If you are a gambler and losing; or a hustler and getting locked up; this is a poor example of a provider and will not be acceptable for any man.

I hear some of you say, "well you gotta do what you gotta do". Brothers, if you have to do things that can threaten your freedom or the freedom of your family then this is not considered being a good provider. Being a provider should give you a feeling of pride and respect not cause you to be hustling and begging.

Men, there is no getting around it or sugar-coating it. You must be a provider for your home and to your family. Don't live with people and you're not trying to pay any bills or not carrying your own weight as a grown ass man. Do not constantly borrow from people, do not steal or fail to repay your obligations to people. This is not being a man in any form or fashion.

The message here is to constantly work at being a provider day in and day out until you get it right, and do not be afraid to work at McDonald's to pay the bills. Do not hesitate at cleaning bathrooms or throwing newspapers to be a better provider. You must do all that it takes to take care of your home and your family.

Men Are Spiritual Leaders

This is a tough one guys.

You say how can we be tough and rugged and be spiritual leaders? We even may like to fight and brawl, but how can we be spiritual leaders? Well it just is, my brothers.

This can be difficult for a lot of you, but no matter what your faith is, the bottom line is that our family, our mates, and our children follow the spiritual lead of the man.

If you want to have good relationships and good families then you must lead spiritually. This means you must follow some sort of spiritual power and belief system. It's crucial that the women and children follow our lead. You can be a strong rugged man and love and serve God. You can be a fighter and be rough around the edges and love God or whomever your maker is.

I definitely do not want to exclude any religions out here, but for myself God is my spiritual leader. If you have some sort of spiritual guidance men this makes you even stronger and powerful because mentally you will not be persuaded to do dumb stuff and make dumb decisions. Not only that, your friends, family, and children will respect you even more when you can teach and lead them spiritually.

So my brothers, I beg you, please find someone in your faith to teach you and guide you spiritually so your life won't be a bunch of crap.

Men Are Humble Servants

Okay my brothers here is the part that may be difficult for some of you--humility. Humility is the ability to have pride, be thankful, and not let it get to your head and cause you to act like an asshole.

Being humble is the foundation to being a great leader in your life. Being thankful for what you have and what you have been through will help you be a better person.

Now for some of you, you may not have a lot and you may have been through hell, but the good part is that you can be humble about it and understand that you can--and will--be better in the long run.

People are attracted to humble men. You can be confident, strong, and a ladies' man and still be a humble person. Humble is understanding what you have, and keeping your ego in check. Being arrogant and cocky are okay sometimes, but being humble is good all the time.

If you are walking around like you are God's gift to the world-- that may be attractive for a little while, but believe me that will turn off everyone in a short amount of time. If you are a humble man that knows he is a great person then you will be much more likeable, trusting, and attractive.

Again, some of the greatest leaders in the world were humble servants--Jesus Christ being the best example of them all. Great soldiers, athletes, executives, etc. all become great in their fields because they served humbly. Each man in their industry learned and mastered their skills humbly, and then they were recognized by other humble leaders--which made them the top of their field.

When you are on a team and you do your part to serve your teammates, your teammates see you are humble in your job and they will be willing to follow and serve you whenever the time arrives for you to take charge. But if you are acting cocky and being a hot shot and selfish, then no one will want to follow you. If no one is willing to follow you, then you cannot be a leader, and you are not worthy to lead anyone. Being humble is a character builder and it's a necessary part of you being a real man.

Men Have Fear, But Are Not Fearful

When I was in the military and served in Desert Storm there were times that I was afraid for my life and the life of my comrades.

Real men are allowed to have and feel fear in life.

The real issue comes when you are *always* fearful of doing things in life. Real men cannot be afraid of wanting to take chances, wanting to succeed, or wanting to step out in uncertain territories. We as men are designed to be explorers and adventurers by nature. Fear can paralyze us and even deteriorate our characters to the point where it keeps us from accomplishing the things that God has designed for us to do.

My brothers, in this day and time there are so many men that fear accomplishment; fear commitment; fear being responsible; and fear what people will say about them stepping up for something good and just. It is because of this fear that we have a generation of weaker men. If we continue to operate in fear, then our younger men and boys will grow up to be weaker.

Now, again don't think that you can't be scared about things. It is okay to be scared sometimes. What we need to be concerned about is how we deal with being afraid and making sure we are not living daily in fear.

As men we must learn to put our fears aside and work on overcoming fear and not letting it rule us and make us weak. If you are living a life where you are in constant, daily fear of something brothers, then it is time to talk to someone about it--whether it be your best friend, a pastor, an uncle, or a mentor.

If we discuss it then we can work together to overcome it. Don't feel ashamed--nine times out of ten, all of us have probably had the same fears at some point in our lives.

WHAT MY FATHER NEVER TAUGHT ME

Real Men Learn to Listen

Well my brothers, I thought I would add this section because through the years I learned that to be a great man I had to learn to listen.

All my life people have been telling me things that I needed to do to help me along the way, but when I was younger I seemed to be an okay listener. For a lot of you out there--and I'm talking to the young men here and some older ones--there are people trying to tell you things to help you in your life and some of you are so hard-headed that you don't want to listen.

I don't get it, why is it when someone is telling us something valuable that we are not smart enough to listen?

The answer is because we think we know every damn thing, and believe me men, we do **not** know everything!

The moment we think we know everything is the moment we can declare ourselves an ignorant jackass. Real men ask questions and take notes. Real men listen and think about the information and make educated and smart decisions.

My brothers, I know it's hard to be humble and submit yourselves to listen to other people, but it's so crucial that you understand that listening will make you powerful. Some of the greatest leaders are also the greatest listeners. They became great because they carefully listened to highly intelligent people around them and took that information to help them become successful.

Also men, if you listen to a woman speak she will tell you how to date her and even how to make her happy and keep her. If you are willing to ask questions of your employees or even coworkers then you can become a better employee, manager, or even a better business owner. *It costs you nothing to listen, but it will cost you everything to not listen.*

You can miss out on some great opportunities in your life by not sitting down and listening to business ideas, advice, counseling, your mate, or your children.

Listening is a skill that can and must be developed by each of us. To be a good listener you must learn to be patient and sit back and let people talk. To be a good listener, do not interrupt who is talking. Don't try to quickly assume what they are going to say and attempt to finish their sentences before they do. (Men are notorious for doing this.)

After you listen, take your time and absorb and process what they said before you respond. Usually when you answer too quickly you respond in the wrong way. Men, stop saying stupid stuff without thinking first. Learn and practice listening and taking your time to process, *then* respond to what you are listening to. If you do this my brothers you will be more intelligent and you will sound intelligent.

Okay men, in this first lesson we talked about what a man is and how the world has defined our position. We were created to lead and be the provider and protector of those around us. As men we are here to be the icons of character, pride, humility, honor, and integrity.

We also discussed that it's okay if we did not have a father to teach us who we are and what we are to do as men. This is because as men we should--and will--pull together to teach each other our roles.

Men are destined to be the leaders of the world. It is necessary that we understand that the world follows our examples. We are the ones that will determine the success of our cultures and our generations.

In the next lesson we will talk about how men are to develop and keep good relationships.

So let's get to it...

2ND LESSON: HOW REAL MEN SHOULD DATE & BUILD RELATIONSHIPS

Why Men Date

Okay my brothers, I'm really excited about this lesson on dating and relationships because this is the area that I had the hardest time developing as a man.

It seemed that after I dated my high school sweetheart, it was hit and miss since then until I got it right. I didn't know about this thing called "**courting**", which we also nowadays call "**dating**".

Now men, I'm going to break this down to cover how to properly date, how to find the right mate, and how to keep our new mate to build a successful relationship. I don't care if you are 15 or 65 these principles apply to all men and can produce successful results for all men. As a result, I believe we should be implementing these principles both as a way to produce better men and to help us find better women.

The reason men date is to try to find the right woman who can fulfill our needs for companionship and hopefully, who we one day can join with and create a good marriage that will make us happy.

In this day and time we see divorce at an all-time high—occurring in 50% of all first time marriages and 20% of second marriages.

The problem as I see it is that we as men are first and foremost not being realistic and honest with ourselves about what we want in a relationship; secondly, we are not committing to our decisions to stick with our marriages through our problems, and lastly we simply don't seem to have the knowledge of what it takes to keep our marriages together.

To solve this epidemic problem, we have to look at the root of the problem—and that starts with us (men) as the leader of the relationship. We can blame it on other factors men, and yes, I know that in some occasions it is the woman that has caused problems so that we have had to terminate the relationship, but I want to make sure that as men we do not continue to make the same mistakes and not succeed in our relationships. So here we go.

Brothers, each section in this Lesson is going to take you from start to finish on the principles of dating and successfully finding a good woman--from meeting them, to walking down the aisle in marriage, and building a successful marriage. We can flourish as men and take care of our future sons and daughters so they in turn can be successful. Remember, you are the leader of the household and the relationship so the pressure is always on you to succeed.

Know Who You Are & Know What You Want

Do you like a woman with blond hair, brown hair, or black hair? Does she need to be nicely-tanned, silky-white, brown skin, dark skin, light skin, olive skin? Does she need to be tall at 5'7" or 5'10" or do you prefer 5'0" to 5'5"? Do you like slim, thick, curvy, athletic, or BBW?

Gentlemen do you like a funny woman, an affectionate woman, a family-oriented woman, a party girl, a freak, an exotic woman, a country girl, Indian, Asian, African, European? Does she need to be Jewish, Muslim, Christian, Atheist, etc.?

The fundamental question I'm asking first men is do you know what your preference in a woman is?

I'm not asking what your mother thinks you should like, or what your family thinks you should like. I'm asking what do YOU like?

And if you do not know what you like then this is the start of why you should date. Dating is synonymous with "DISCOVERY". You date to discover what you like and see if you wish to pursue that discovery.

Brothers, to successfully date you need to know who YOU are so you can find the right match. You need to know if you are a professional, a jock, a social icon, or are you a playboy?

Once you know who you are, then you can successfully search for what you need and want and what kind of girl or woman fits your personality. Do you want her loud and edgy? Do you want sexy and flirty? Do you want her wholesome and innocent?

So men let's start being honest. Do you want a woman that is a quiet freak? Do you want a woman that likes threesomes? Or do you want a woman that is religious and conservative?

Whatever you want, be true to yourself and stick to what you want. Don't compromise and don't deviate, unless your taste changes. Then follow what you desire.

So let's walk this process out.

Real Men Take The Initiative

Okay men, here we go. We see a girl or woman that we want to get to know. We find her very attractive and then we find out she has a nice character. The hunter and conqueror inside of us wants to acquire this woman as our mate. So here is where the hunt begins.

Real men take the first step and we approach the woman and introduce ourselves.

Men it is up to you to start the process--not her.

You walk up to her and introduce yourself: 'Hello, my name is "Fearless Man", and I found you very attractive. I would like the opportunity to take you out on a date.'

Then shut up! Wait for the YES!

Men, if she says no, or if she is already dating someone, then say "thank you" and move on to the next conquest. This is all you have to do. You may not be her type, or she may really have a man. Respect the other man that is dating her and move on to a woman that is free. Don't disrespect the guy she is dating.

Real men don't beg!

Never beg for a woman to go out with you. You are a leader and leaders do not have to beg for a date. If she says yes then ask for her number and then you make sure you take the initiative and call her within 24 hours to secure a date and time for a date. This is it men. It's very simple and to the point. No extra talk is needed. Never stand there taking up 20 minutes of her time or else she will have nothing to look forward to and you will talk yourself right out of an opportunity.

My brothers, here is where so many of us miss the mark and mess it all up. Brothers you all fail to call her within 24 to 48 hours of meeting her to secure a date. The woman is waiting for you anxiously to see what type of man you are. She wants to see are you a real man and will take charge and plan a date. As I said earlier real men are leaders and they take charge of a relationship.

Make sure before you call you have something planned that is fun and inexpensive for a date. First dates men should be fun and simple, no extravagant dinners or trips on a first date. Your first date should ALWAYS be in a quiet place where both of you can talk and spend time getting to ask questions and get to know one another. Don't do loud concerts, loud movies, or go to a party. First dates should be a nice café, bistro, the park, the zoo, the mall. Anywhere you can walk and talk, or sit and talk.

Now, this goes without saying, but make sure you have money to actually go on a date. Although it should not be an expensive first date, you should have enough money to get ice cream, coffee, cotton candy, a hotdog or hamburger, IHOP, or Applebee's. For safety reasons your first date should never exceed $40. You don't want to carry a lot of cash unnecessarily.

Try not to exceed 3 or 4 hours for a date. This is long enough. If you plan it correctly it should be fun and affordable. You should always be on a dating budget and try never to exceed the budget. Now let's break this down even further on the proper habits of a man when dating.

Personal Hygiene

Brothers, bad breath is NEVER an option for anyone, especially on a date. Make sure you brush your teeth every time you meet a woman. If you have breath problems then start brushing your teeth and flossing, also use a strong mouth wash. Wal-Mart has great mouthwash for extra bad breath.

Next, make sure on every date you chew and carry chewing gum or have breath mints. Never go out without having chewing gum with you. You never know if you will get that evening kiss, and you always want to be ready for anything. A woman will be more comfortable to want to kiss you if she knows you have fresh breath. Also, make sure you carry lip balm with you. No woman wants to see or kiss dry lips. This is definitely a turn off for every woman.

Gentlemen, always shower and bathe before you go out. No woman wants to smell your body odor. Never meet a woman when you just finished working out, or right after you got off work all day. Always be fresh and clean when you go to meet a woman. Again, a woman will be more comfortable to be close to you and touch you if you are smelling fresh and clean. Also, my brothers make sure you wear a nice, soft smelling, light cologne. I advise that you ask women around you what colognes that they like. Don't choose your own cologne.

Take a careful note here. The cologne is to attract the woman not yourself. She is the one who wants to smell you. Cologne makes you more attractive and appealing to the opposite sex, so it only makes sense that the opposite sex should pick your cologne. You don't have to pay top dollar for a good cologne. You can go to the Dollar Store and buy a knock off of a cologne for little or nothing. Be smart men, cologne is only scented water. If you are on a budget, an inexpensive cologne is just as good as an expensive one. When you can afford a more expensive one then feel free to get one.

Now, let's talk about your clothes. Men I see some terrible looking outfits out there and I'm hoping that you are not one of those tragic examples. Let's do some fashion policing here. Make sure your clothes are ironed and wrinkle-free. You look like you don't care about your appearance when your clothes are wrinkled and be sure the colors of your outfit match.

As a man you should try and dress up for a first date, and really you should dress up on all dates. "Dressing up" means shirt, jeans, belt, and casual or dress shoes in addition to a decent sweater or sports coat.

Stop going out with tee shirts and jeans with holes in them. And be sure to wear socks and decent shoes. Never go out on a first date in sneakers or tennis shoes. This is definitely a no, no!

Wear black or brown shoes and a belt with your pants that match the color of the shoes. This is very easy men. Do it! You should always dress to impress her. If you do not have a decent outfit then you need to go out and borrow a jacket and a dress shirt or go buy one from Ross, JCPenny or Sears. Men always wear black socks with dress shoes or casual shoes. Only wear white socks with white sneakers and tennis shoes.

Lastly, men your hair and face should always look clean. If you wear a beard make sure it is shaped up nice and not all bushy and unkept. If you have a lot of hair make sure it is washed and combed, or brushed nicely. If you have out of control hair then get a damn haircut. Stop wearing these outrageous, crazy looking hairdos!

Brothers, women want a man they can be proud of in public--not a clown that everyone stares at. You should always look presentable and manly.

This section is specifically meant for all my young brothers when it comes to dressing in public and for a date.

Never go out in public with your pants sagging around your behind and showing your underwear. Young brothers, sagging pants came from gay men in prison who sagged their pants to let other men poke them in the rear. Men, I do not like that rappers are dressing this way, idolizing prison styles. This is ridiculous and immature. I also see grown men over 30 years old dressing this way. Men this is definitely unacceptable! Dressing like homosexual inmates is not cool. It looks like you are inviting other men to poke you in the butt.

I know I am being harsh by talking about the new style in this way, but believe me my brothers, this style is not cool in any way. I also am telling you that no girl or woman wants to go out with any man that has pants hanging off his butt like he constantly wants to be poked in the butt. Grow up men and start dressing like a grown man. I cannot and will not respect men that wear sagging pants.

Enough of that, I hope and pray that all of you heed these tips on being great men that will go out on great dates.

Real Men Open Doors Always

Now I'm not quite sure where the ritual started on opening doors for our women, but what I do know is that it shows respect for the woman and shows a romantic side that women want to see. It starts first with opening the door for our mothers, our sisters, and our daughters. We should start teaching our sons to open doors for women as soon as they learn to walk and hold a door open. Usually, that is at age 6 and 7. This shows respect to women and teaches boys to be strong and polite. In turn, women will have a great deal of respect for us as men. It's a mutual requirement and need for both men and woman.

Brothers make sure you are opening the doors to the restaurants, and opening the doors to the malls and drug stores. Also, make sure that you open the car doors for women when getting in and out of the car. This is what real men do. And believe me, a woman will respect you as a real man when you start doing this all the time.

Real Men Pull Out Seats

Okay men, this is important both while you're on a date and in your general interactions with women. When you go to a restaurant it is good manners that you pull a woman's seat out from the table. Then, let her stand in front of the chair and as she sits down you gently push the chair under her legs until she sits down. When she sits down let her pull her own seat in under the table.

Don't make this a big deal but make sure you are practicing this every time there is a chair at a table that you can pull out for her. This will win you great points with a woman. Again, it shows being respectful, romantic, and that you have good manners, and that you are a great guy.

Order Her Food

Men when you sit down look at the menu and have a great conversation with her and find out what she would like to try and what she wants to eat. Say, "Have you found something that you want to try"? When she says yes, ask what she wants and make sure you remember it. When the server comes you make sure you order her drink, and order her food when ready. Make sure you know what she wants to drink, what she wants as an appetizer, and what she wants to eat as the main dinner.

When the food is served gentlemen make sure you check with her and see if her order is correct. If it is not correct make sure you nicely take the initiative with the server to get it corrected and make sure that it is right. This shows her that you are concerned and that you can take charge to make sure things are right. When you do this men she will automatically feel secure.

Pay The Bill

Men this is important. When the bill comes make sure you double-check the bill to make sure that you are charged for the items you ordered and that the amount is correct. Make sure you tip the server. A tip amount can range anywhere from 10% to 20%. If it was poor then 10% is the minimum. If service was okay then 15% to 20% or more is acceptable.

Never discuss the bill or show the bill to your date. It is not her business what you paid for the dinner. And never let the woman pay for the first date, or even a second date. I know we are in different times. If after 3 or 4 dates she asks to pay for the date then let her if you wish. If she does not ever ask then understand that as the man you are responsible for paying for the date.

This is why men you want to take the initiative to always plan a date so you can stay within a reasonable budget. There are many, many things that you can plan inexpensively for a good date.

Don't ever leave her with the bill and make sure men that you always go to eat at a place where you can always pay for the most expensive thing if she asks for it.

Never use your bill money or rent money to pay for a date. Men, if you cannot pay for the date then plan the date when you do have extra money. Never be afraid to stay on a budget and stick to it. If she is a good woman then she will understand that you are financially responsible and that you want to stay within your budget.

Now if she volunteers to want to pay for the date, then let her only if you are comfortable with her doing so. Remember when you are dating this is the test and that women are observing to see if you are a good provider. As much as you might want to impress her, never, break your pockets and spend beyond your means for a date.

Always remember to be creative. You can always cook a meal at home and rent movies if you are on a tight budget. Also, you can invite her over for dinner and a board game.

Giving Her Gifts

Men, I must say that I do not advise giving gifts to a woman on the first date. You can get flowers, but make sure you know exactly what type of flowers she likes, and be sure that she even likes flowers. There are women that are allergic to certain flowers, or just don't like flowers at all. This is why I would hold off on flowers and gifts until after a first date when you can converse with her and find out what exactly she likes.

Also, giving a gift to a woman on a first date shows that you are too anxious, or desperate, or that you are trying to buy her. If you do this it will give her the wrong message that she is some sort of "hoe" and that she is easy or you can buy her affection.

Men, this is not a good move to buy her gifts too early. I advise you to not buy any woman gifts until you have established that you are in a committed relationship. Brothers, by holding off on buying gifts, it really gives you a chance to see what type of woman she is. Is she just with you because of the gifts, or does she really like you for you?

Never Honk The Horn And Always Walk Her To The Door

Brothers, I have a daughter and I never want a boy or man to drive up to my doorstep and honk the horn for my daughter to come running out of the house like you are a taxi cab. Men, never honk the horn for a lady when you are just dating. Be a real man and park the car and come to the door and knock politely to pick her up. This is a classy move and it's a mature move. It again shows leadership and lets her know that you are a protector.

When it is the end of the date make sure you open her door before she gets out of the car and walk her to the door of the house or apartment to make sure she gets in safely. Again, this shows class, good manners, and that you are a strong protector.

Remember men, she is following your lead and observing you to see if you are a real man that she may want to date regularly. It's very important that you do this on a regular basis. Always walk a woman to her door to make sure she gets in safely, plus you never know--if you do it enough times she may just feel comfortable to invite you in.

Great Conversation Goes a Long Way

My brothers, this is probably one of the most important sections that we may ever discuss. What you talk about and how you talk about things will not only make you successful on your date, but it will make you successful in life.

When on a date, a girl or a grown woman wants to feel like she is important and the center of attention. Here is precisely where your listening skills will be most important. When talking to a woman on a date, make sure you focus your questions on her. "Where are you from originally? How did you grow up? What things do you like to do for fun? What makes you happy? What makes you sad?"

This is the point that you find out the things that she likes and what is important in her life. What is her favorite color? Does she like her parents? Where does she go to church? I know men, it may sound a bit boring, but I assure you that the woman will appreciate this, and she will find you caring and appealing.

Now here is a key point men---you want to answer the same questions yourself for her. By doing this, this will start to make your conversations fun and interesting.

Special note here men--DO NOT TALK ABOUT SEX ON YOUR FIRST DATE!

Okay, you say. "But Shawn what if she talks about it?" Men, there is nothing wrong with a little flirting, but do your best to be the leader and stay in control. You guide the conversation. If she has a question about something sexual tell her, " Now you know you are not ready for all that". Of course, this will sound flirty and interesting but it will keep you in control.

Men, women are merely testing you to see if you are a dog, or a snake and only want sex. Whether you do or don't my brothers, don't get weak and lose your position by letting her take you down this road too early. Shift the conversation back to questions and answers-- anything from fashion, to politics, to sports--but do not talk sex on a first date.

Next gentlemen, if she is attractive you can compliment her on her dress, her hair, her makeup, but ONLY DO THAT ONCE ON THE DATE! Don't become obsessive and tell her 50 times how beautiful she is. I promise you if you do that over and over again it will turn her off and you will lose the chance for a second date.

Remember attractive women know they are attractive and hear it all the time. If you say it once on the date she knows you are sincere. If you keep repeating it, then she will think you are a stalker, a pervert or only after one thing.

Men, when you are talking to a woman or anyone during a conversation, it is very, very important that you look them in the eyes when you are talking to them. Making direct eye contact shows confidence. You always want to try and be confident when you are talking to people. Confidence also shows intelligence and competence. These are qualities that leaders have and you always want to work on building leadership skills.

Brothers when you are talking to a woman during a conversation do not be arrogant or cocky. You can be confident but do not boast about how much money you make, what type of car you drive, or drop names about what famous people you know. Woman love a man that is humble but confident.

They also love a man that can share how he feels about something and can be funny and tell GOOD jokes. Gentleman, try hard to not be so nervous and uptight when talking to women. Also, make sure you smile when you are talking. Don't make mean or unpleasant faces. Women feel comfortable with you when you smile and laugh.

Also, respect a woman if she has an opinion about something that is different than your views. You can have a friendly conversation about the issues but NEVER argue or criticize her views. If you argue with a woman on a first or even a second date you can guarantee that will be your last date.

Make sure you say "please" and "thank you" when it is appropriate. Women like a polite and well-mannered man. This will always make you appear strong and sexy to her. Again, make sure you pause and allow her to respond to your questions and comments. Do not cut her off when she is talking if possible. And make sure you are actually listening to what she says so you can respond correctly and not give a stupid response.

Men if you follow some of these helpful tips not only will you be good at conversing with women, but you will be great at conversing with anyone at anytime.

P.D.A (Public Displays of Affection)

Okay my brothers, this is important. Women like different degrees of showing affection in public. I'm going to discuss these types of affection and show you how these can work to your advantage.

First, men when you are walking down a street--I mean any street--make sure that you are always walking along the curb side where the cars are driving. Since early British times it was considered honorable to walk along side of the road between the carriages and the woman to protect the woman from horses and carriages that may swerve and hit her. Again, this portrays you as being a protector, men.

Nowadays, of course, we do not see a lot of carriages, but we do have cars along the street, so it is now chivalrous to walk on the curbside between the cars and the lady you are walking with. Make sure men you are doing this all the time, and teaching your sons to do the same.

Secondly, let's talk about holding hands in public. Men, I know a lot of you do not always like to do this in public. There is absolutely nothing wrong with holding the woman's hand in public. Now, if you are not attracted to her or there is clearly not a romantic interest, then I advise you to not do this.

Also, this can be tricky when you are first getting to date a woman. You need to find out if she likes holding hands in public. I have met some women in my past that do not like doing that, but it is safe to assume that MOST women really do like holding hands in public. Holding hands shows that you like her, and she feels secure and protected by you. I assure you if you are hesitant or scared to hold hands in public, then she will find some other man that will. So my brothers, man up and start holding hands in public.

The third issue I'll address is kissing in public. Now this is more of a personal preference. My brothers, it is totally up to you if you are comfortable to kiss in public view. I do not think there is anything wrong with doing that, but I do recommend that you do not have a "suck face fest" in public and behave inappropriately. If you want to kiss and hold each other for long periods of time I suggest that you find a private area. Take it to your house or her house. That's all I have to say on this one my brothers.

Talking About Sex

My brothers this is also a crucial point in the success of dating. Talking about sex on a first date is often a no-no. Now, let's talk about why. As men, we are physical beings and enjoy sex--or at least most men do. Women already know that we are like this, so there is no need to go over the top convincing her to have sex.

I was told a long, long time ago that in the first 30 seconds of meeting a woman she will know if you are someone that she wants to have sex with. To confirm that decision she will know if you are a candidate for sex after a first date. If the first date is good then she will just be observing you until she decides she is ready for that experience. So, what I'm telling you men is that if you don't say something stupid and ignorant then you are okay in that area. Women who are continuing to date you are in essence saying "yes we can have sex" (at some point when she is ready—not when you pressure her to do it), until you do something to mess it up. The key here is to try hard to not mess it up and just wait patiently. I assure you that time will come when both of you are ready.

Now, I would be wrong to not properly tell our young men that it would be great as a Christian man to wait until you find the right woman, marry her, and then have sex. Men, I'm not here to preach to you but I would not be a true mentor or a help to you if I did not discuss the plan that God has for each and every young strong man out here.

Let's look at this men, if we just were to wait to find a good girl and wait until we were married to have sex, we may start to eliminate this epidemic of creating young dads that cannot take care of their children. I'm just saying this is something to really think about.

I encourage you to start relationships with a woman and take the time to enjoy knowing her personality and hold off on sex. The problem is that we are too often letting our sexual needs control us as primitive animals—but we are not barbaric animals men. We are intelligent and responsible leaders. But, I'm keeping it real here my brothers--if you give in to your sexual desires, then the least I ask is to be responsible men.

Being responsible men means to try and at least hold off after a few dates and some quality time before you have sex. My brothers if you do have sex then have RESPONSIBLE SEX! This means using condoms.

There are all types of condoms that women like to use--Trojans,

Lifestyles, Magnums, ultra-sensitive for maximum pleasure, and there are numerous others that I encourage men to try and become familiar with.

Men—here's a special note--always, always be prepared and have condoms with you if you are sexually active. Keep them in your car, in your coat pockets but NOT IN YOUR WALLETS! When you keep them in your wallet they dry out and you risk having a BAD CONDOM!

Also men, try not to have your lady give you condoms. The problem here is that they might not be good enough to use or they could have been tampered with. Just keeping it real men, there are women out here that tamper with condoms to make you think you are protected and then you end up with an unwanted baby.

Let's not be stupid men, carry your own condoms so you have secure peace of mind and you are being responsible at all times. Remember men you do not want to be that irresponsible father who does not want to take care of your baby.

Guys, you should also wear condoms because STDs (Sexually Transmitted Diseases) are growing rampant. There is a dangerously growing number of HIV/AIDS cases among men. You can also contract herpes, the clap, yeast infections, etc. from unprotected sex. Men, this is real crap you cannot get rid of easily and women do not want to be with a man that has a sexual disease. Plus, some of these diseases and infections can put your woman and a baby at risk. There is absolutely no reason to have sex unprotected. Remember men you are leaders, protectors, and we make the world go round. We were made to procreate but not with diseases.

So my brothers, hold off on discussing sex on the first date. You can flirt with the idea, but women are waiting for you to slip up and see if you are a shallow dog, or a playboy. Even if you are one, you still need to respect the situation and hold off on that subject.

Take the first date as an initial interview. Find out what she is about, what she likes and doesn't like, what are her goals, her interests. Find out if she is intelligent or stupid, responsible or irresponsible. Hell, after the first date you may find out you do not want to have sex with her or even see her again. Leave that door closed until a later time. I promise you if you hold that discussion it will come to you in due time.

Dress for Dating Success

Men just like you must dress a certain way for a job interview, dating is exactly the same thing--a relationship interview.

Here are my suggestions on acceptable fashion for a date. The way you look for a date shows the woman the level of respect you have for her. If you dress nicely and are presentable it shows her you care enough about her and her reaction. This is no different than when a woman gets dressed up and sexy for you. It clearly shows you that she wants you to feel respected and that you will be highly attracted to her.

So men I usually say to try and avoid wearing jeans for a first date. Casual slacks are preferred, but you can wear nice clean jeans on rare occasions. Wear some khaki, blue, or black pants. No shorts on a date. Then men I advise you to wear a nice, pressed button-down shirt---long-sleeve if the weather is cool, or a polo shirt is also okay.

Now, if you can, I feel if you want to wear a nice, casual blazer jacket over your shirt then do so. This gives you a touch of class and swag men. Women love classy and stylish. A tan jacket, dark blue or black is preferred.

As for shoes--never wear sneakers or tennis shoes on a first date as I stated earlier in the book. And, if you wear dress or casual shoes ALWAYS WEAR BLACK SOCKS! Never wear white socks with dress shoes. Also, your belt should always match the color of your shoes.

Never go on a date with your shirt not tucked into your pants. A shirt out of the pants is SLOPPY! Also make sure your shoes are clean and not busted or worn out. If you need to, get some new casual shoes at Wal-Mart or Payless, or invest in some really nice brown or black shoes from a men's store.

The point here is to look as good as you would going to an interview or going to church. There are no tee-shirts worn on a date. Last, but not least, make sure your nose hairs are not long and showing out of your nose, make sure your fingernails are cut nicely and clean and that you are freshly shaved or have your hair cut. Last, remember no bad breath or chapped lips.

Now you are ready for a great date!

The Chariot of Warriors

Okay my brothers this is a funny section where I'll be talking about your transportation. Yes, this is about your car, your truck, or motorcycle, etc. When you pick up your date, make sure your vehicle is clean and working properly. Also, make sure you gas up before the date.

The inside of your vehicle is a representation of who you are. If your car is junky most likely your home or room is junky, and men, women do not feel comfortable in a junky car. Try to make sure the outside of your car is clean also.

Men, I understand that times are hard and you may not have your car because of financial reasons, but let me keep it real here. It is not cool to have a woman pick you up and drive you around, especially for a date. If you need to borrow a car then do it, hell if you need to rent a car then do it. But, if for some reason you do have the woman pick you up then make sure you offer to pay for gas for her car. A real man makes sure he offers to put gas in her car or even fill it up if you are able to. This will show her you are considerate and that you can be a good provider.

Brothers it is the role of a real man to drive. It is important that you always drive and pick up your lady, it is also important that if you are using her car then, at least, offer to drive her car so she does not have to. Now be careful here, some women do not want you to drive their car so be ready if she declines your offer. The point here is that you at least offered.

I'm so tired of seeing men always riding on the passenger side of the car when they should be driving. If your license is suspended or revoked, then handle your business and get it taken care of men. No woman feels you are a good potential mate if you cannot even get your license straight.

The End of the Date

Okay brothers, hopefully you had a successful and fun date getting to know the woman of your dreams. Hopefully, she laughed, you asked her all about herself, and she feels like she was the only one in the room.

During the course of the date you should have found out if she enjoyed herself and if she is open to seeing you again. If the vibe is right and the date was properly executed then all you need to do is CLOSE THE DEAL!

You take her home or to her car, then when she is about to get into her vehicle or her home, stop her and tell her that you really enjoyed the date and that you would like to see her again soon. Men soon means within the next 7 days. Then ASK HER, "Can I take you on another date in the future?" Her answer should be yes. Thank her for her time and let her know again that she looked beautiful today. Men, you have now CLOSED THE DEAL.

Now, make sure that you take the initiative and plan the next date. Make sure there are a series of phone calls to follow up with her and make sure you are growing the relationship until the next date. This is dating men. It's merely going from date to date until you ask her to be in a relationship. That's right, I said ASK HER TO BE IN A RELATIONSHIP. We will discuss this later on about men building and leading successful relationships.

Men, I want to tell all of you that if you follow these tips on dating, I assure you that you will be highly successful in creating good relationships. These tips are not the solutions to having a perfect relationship, but at least you will be doing the right things in dating to show that you have manners, pride, and respect for women.

By showing the woman you are dating that you have manners and respect for her, she will be compelled to have respect for you. If she does not show you mutual respect then this will be a clear indicator that SHE IS NOT THE ONE FOR YOU!

Happy dating men!.

3RD LESSON: REAL MEN TEACH, MENTOR & RAISE THEIR BOYS

Real Men Raise Their Children

Okay my brothers, open your ears wide here I'm going to touch some nerves in this section, but regardless I need you to Man Up and take this.

60% of American homes are raising children without their fathers. The good news is that the remaining 40% are successfully raising their children with fathers in the home, or are single dads raising their children. I applaud you my brothers that are raising their children at home.

Let's understand this gentlemen--there are many of you out here who have left your children because the relationship with your ex-girlfriend did not work, or your relationship with your ex-wife did not work out, or you had a one night stand. I can't say that you are, or are not justified to have left your children. The bottom line is that we still have men who are not inside of the home that need to be there. Men this is not what God intended for us to do as leaders, as protectors, or as providers. I cannot stress to you how crucial it is that you raise your children whether they are at home with you or not.

A lot of you men out here are not speaking to your children or not involved with your children because you are mad at the mother for leaving you, or maybe she was stupid and you had to leave her. Regardless, the only one who is suffering majorly is your child or your children. Men I need you all to get your heads out of your ass and grow the hell up and start taking care of your seeds. Now, if you are not sure if that is your child or children, GET A D.N.A TEST DONE! If you are a real leader you will get it done so you know the truth and take care of your responsibilities.

Brothers, your children never asked to be here on this planet. You helped to make them and place them here, so as a real man it is your job to take care and protect them. Now brothers **IT IS YOUR RESPONSIBILITY TO PAY CHILD SUPPORT**. This is not a request or a question for your personal opinion. I think it's a shame and it's pathetic that the law has to make a grown man take care of his child or children. Men, if you cannot pay, then find a way to pay. You do whatever it is you must do LEGALLY to support your child. If you need to have two jobs then do it, start your own business and do it. This whole thing of quitting your job to avoid taking care of your children is crazy, but men are doing it and it is pathetic.

Real Men Raise Their Boys

Brothers your sons need you! I cannot say this any simpler. Your son needs you to be a dad to him because this is how he learns everything from how to pee in the toilet, to how he should talk and walk. Your son wants to imitate his dad because we all want to be just like our dads. If you are not there then who will he imitate? Do you want your son imitating his mother? Do you want him imitating his male coach? Do you want him imitating his mother's boyfriend? Or do you want him imitating YOU?

Do you understand men that it is so important that you raise your boy to be a Prince, and to ultimately raise him to be a King? But, if you are acting like a clown then how can your son have a real chance to be a man? He can't and he won't, all because you are not there.

Now how do we start to fix this, men? First, we have to accept that we have not been the best father to our children and decide that you want to do better. Are you willing to confront this and decide that you can and will do better? I hope so, because if you do not do this then your son or sons are lost.

Second, you have to decide that you are going to commit yourself to doing better at wanting to communicate with your children. After you make this commitment you have to tell someone, tell your friends, your girlfriend, your mother or your father that you decided to be a better dad to your children. By doing this my brothers you will have someone who can help you be accountable for your actions. Being "accountable" means they will check in with you daily, weekly, or monthly to support you and encourage you to being a better dad.

Please do not think that reconnecting with your kids is easy. It's not, so I don't want to lie to you, I want to prepare you for the challenge. Men, the mothers of your children will be angry with you, they will try to ignore you, and they will threaten you and say that you better not come into their children's lives and hurt them by going in and out of their lives.

Men you must understand that it will be a long and tiring journey to reconnect with your children, but it is so worth it. Your kids will love you for fighting to be with them, and you will be happy that you will be their father and the leader you are supposed to be. Men you only have one life to live and you better live it and take care of your children and raise your boys.

Men Teach Your Sons

Men you are conquerors, you are leaders, and you are all kings. Many of you are blessed to have young princes and princesses. Men it is so important that we begin as early as possible to teach our sons how to be a man.

Your role is to teach him to be strong, be responsible, to protect, how to play hard, walk tall, and don't back down. Your role is to teach him how to fix things, how to talk, and how to make sure he is not bullied in school, and how to talk to a young lady.

It is your responsibility to take care of him and teach your son to be a man. Men your son is the only one that can carry your name down from generation to generation. The question is how do you want to be remembered as a father and as a dad both now and to the next generation?

Men Mentor Other Young Men

My brothers, mentoring is a much needed but infrequent art form of teaching. Mentoring is taking a young man by the hand and teaching him the things that he needs about how to be a successful man.

To my young brothers I want you to know that it is very, very important to find and get a mentor. A mentor will be someone older who is intelligent, responsible, and can be a good teacher. A mentor can be anyone in your community that has a good reputation.

Men we need to teach our young men values, respect, loyalty, and leadership. This does not mean getting into a gang is a place to get mentored. Gangs do not have good leaders, they do not have good values, they get no real respect and no one is truly loyal. Real men do not steal from their brothers or kill their brothers.

Mentoring is about respecting other men and people, and teaching them to live better and in a positive and successful manner. Men, I am challenging you to mentor one young boy, or even to mentor another man. Maybe a boy in your neighborhood or in a school mentoring program, or you could mentor a young man at your job, or take a young executive under your wing at your company. As men we need to create other leaders to take our place and develop other strong men.

Boys Need To Belong

Men, we all belong to someone, somewhere. We all have a father somewhere, a mother somewhere, an aunt, an uncle, a grandparent.

Some of us belonged to foster care, or a group home. Some of us were adopted. Either way, all of us as young boys belonged somewhere. When boys act out it is because there is a need to belong. We want and need to belong somewhere as boys and as men. If boys cannot belong somewhere then we will be lost and we will be in major trouble in our lives. This is why it is so important that as fathers we need to make sure we let our sons know they belong to us. Men, we need to communicate with our sons and let them know who they are and where they belong because all boys need to belong to someone.

Boys Need A Team

It doesn't matter if it's a baseball team, a football team, the debate team, the Key Club, the band or a Spelling Bee team--all young men need to be a part of a team. Being on a team is what creates competitiveness and leadership in young men.

Also, being on a team helps boys to socialize with others and to have somewhere where they belong and fit in. Remember, boys need a positive team or group to belong to, not a gang. Again, a gang is not positive and it only tears down our young men. Make sure we are putting our young men on a team in school, or at the local YMCA, or at the local church.

Young Men Need Encouragement

I'd like to say to all my brothers--when raising, teaching, and mentoring our sons it is so important that we are encouraging our young men to succeed. Encouragement is the verbalization of telling them that you are proud of them when they do something good. It is also telling them that you love them. As men so often we don't have the conversations with our sons that let them know we truly love them. We must explicitly say that to our sons because that is how they gain a sense of belonging and feel validation as a boy. Our mothers are good at telling us that they love us, but it is so important that you are telling your sons this as well.

Encouragement is also being there for our sons and being involved in their lives. It means taking them to football, baseball, basketball or soccer practice. When our boys see their fathers come to a male sporting event they feel encouraged and proud. If you ever notice they play harder, they work harder, they appear more dedicated and focused because they want to please their fathers. Men if you need to leave work early or be a volunteer on their teams you need to do whatever it takes to make our sons feel supported and encouraged through your presence and your words.

I know many of you men out here have grown up with dads that did not express love to you. I know in your minds that this was a manly way of loving you, but I'm here to tell you that, this is not the best way to encourage and develop our sons. We NEED TO EXPRESS LOVE to our sons by communication, involvement and teaching them what they need to be strong and succeed. So, perhaps your father did not tell you that he loved you but you need to break this GENERATIONAL CURSE and begin telling your sons you love them, tell them often and encourage them whenever you can.

Disciplining Our Young Men

Over the years I have observed numerous ways that mothers and fathers have disciplined our young men. First, I must say that this is definitely where our dads are greatly needed to help mold and shape our young men. Discipline of boys should come from another male. I know this sounds narrow minded, but please hear me out.

I do not take anything away from strong mothers that have to raise our boys, but I'm here to keep it real! Young lions need to be disciplined by big strong male lions. In nature the male lion teaches his male cub to protect, to fight, and to hunt. This is how they remain King of the Jungle. Men if you are not disciplining our young men then they will be on the road to being rowdy, ill-mannered, and deviant. This is not something I'm making up, this is what society has shown time and time again. So let's talk about how men should discipline our young cubs.

Men, first of all, it starts with being involved with your boys and being consistent. You cannot discipline a boy if you are not constantly involved or "in the know" regarding things in his life. This means you either are there speaking with your son daily if you are in the home, or speaking to mom on a consistent basis about what's going on with your son if you are outside the home.

You have to be constantly aware of his behavior so you will know how you will discipline your son or sons. This means being aware of his grades, his behavior in school, and his behavior at home. This is just like a military operation. First you need adequate intelligence to formulate a plan of attack—which is done once you gather ALL the information. Men, this is a habit that you need to make sure you master--gathering all information before you react. Do not assume you know everything! Make sure you get all of the important intelligence, just like a special agent. Once you have the full story, only then can you move to our plan of attack for good discipline.

The first step in disciplining your son is to setup a moment with no interruptions and tell him that you need to talk to him. The important thing here is that whenever you discipline him that you do it the same way every time.

I suggest the "Fast and Hard" method. The "fast" part of this method means that as soon as you find out what the problem is and you quickly gather the information that you respond quickly to the problem. I say within the hour if possible, or at most the same day. Boys have to be addressed quickly about what they do wrong. You have to be fast.

Responding "hard" means talking to him in a deep, strong, and assertive voice. This does not always mean yelling. Now yelling may work sometimes, but to have it be and remain effective, you should only yell when the infraction is a major one.

When you discipline your son state what the problem is, make sure he understands what the issue is, then give him a moment to respond and then you have to *listen* to his response. Men, a lot of us let our tempers get the best of us and we fail to stop and listen to our children. It is imperative that you stop and listen even when you are angry. Boys need to feel like their feelings and responses matter. After they respond then you can tell them how you feel as a dad--that you are mad, disappointed, etc. After that, you tell him what his punishment is.

Now men I cannot tell you if spanking or physically disciplining your son is proper or not. I would like to say that hopefully your son is not so bad or ill-mannered that you feel the need to whip him constantly. Hopefully you don't have to resort to that at all. There is a very fine line between discipline and abuse, which I will talk about later on in the book.

I am a proponent of spanking, because boys are physical by nature and words backed up with a good spanking linger longer in their minds. The same goes for whipping but some men, let's be real, do not know what the limit is. So, the bottom line here is if your deep voice, and you responding "fast and hard" are not working, and a good spanking is not working then I must say another plan of action to solve disciplinary problems with your son needs to be investigated more deeply.

I would strongly recommend that family counseling come into play here. I say this because there may be some deep-rooted problems that go beyond you being able to discipline him on your own. Men let's not play dumb here. There are boys out here that are totally out of control. Some of these boys may have deep-rooted self-esteem issues, some may have some sort of chemical imbalance, but if we ignore these problems then our sons will have serious problems later in life. If you are involved and you are listening to your sons you will be able to recognize and understand these problems earlier and have a better plan of attack when it comes to discipline.

The Punishments For Young Men

Okay men, there are a lot of creative ways to discipline our young men. Here, I'm going to mention a few creative options that you can use and even put your own twist to them. All of your punishments should encourage discipline and enhance the strength of you as the Head, the Leader.

One punishment is performing military exercises. I love having a young man do push-ups, leg extensions across the yard, doing up-downs, etc. I also recommend having him hold a bag of potatoes in both arms extended straight out ahead of him and then place the bag across his arms and have him stand there for 5 minutes.

I believe in doing chores, such as mowing your yard and ten neighbors' yards for free. Make him wash your car and the neighbors' cars. If he is younger (ages from 2 to 5 years old) then talking to him and taking away his favorite toys for a nominal amount of time works well. Making him go to bed earlier than normal works well, or letting him sit in a chair in the corner for 5 or 10 minutes also works well.

The idea here gentlemen is that if you have a few well thought out punishments and you stay consistent and move quickly, you can handle discipline issues quite easily, plus you can have fun while building up your sons.

Remember, be consistent with your sons and be involved. Remember to get all the information about the situation first--never assume you know everything. Remember to listen and hear your son out. Listen to his feelings, he may be trying to tell you something through his acting out, so do not be afraid to dig deeper with questions and play the role of investigative agent. Remember to respond "Fast and Hard" by reacting within the hour or within 24 hours at the most. Remember to speak with a deep, strong, and assertive voice and have your punishment ready. Men I assure you that if you discipline consistently then you will be ensuring that you will build strong and well-mannered men.

Real Men Take Care of Other Children

Okay brothers, this is a very, very sensitive issue for thousands of men around the world. I want to address this area because it's brutally important that we clear this up if you are struggling with whether you should be taking care of other children outside of your relationship. So, let's get to it.

So you met a young woman and she has a son or sons or children already. At this point if you decide to pursue a relationship with her you must understand that she is a package deal. This means you must think about reaching a point that you will take responsibility for *all* of her children. This means to take care of them morally and financially. If you have a child with her and she has another child, you need to consider treating both children the same and love them both the same if you are in a relationship with her. Real men are protectors, leaders, and providers. If you are man enough to have sex with this woman then you should be man enough to take care of her children. Children do not decide who their parents are. So as a head of the household this means the children are under your watch. You are responsible, bottom line!

Now Shawn, what if my wife or girlfriend cheated and had another child by another man, do I need to care for that child also? This is a difficult decision, but it is within you to decide. If you are man enough to take her back and forgive her, then you need to be able to love that child. Again, if you are the head of the household, the leader in the relationship, then you must be prepared to take care of all children involved and DO NOT TREAT THE CHILDREN DIFFERENTLY, LOVE ALL THE CHILDREN THE SAME!

Real Men Teach Our Young Men To Pray

Prayer, my brothers, is the thing that keeps us warriors on the straight, narrow and righteous path. How can you be a good provider, protector and leader if you do not have the necessary moral values and integrity? You can't.

No matter what your faith is, it is very important that you as the leader and teacher of your sons teach them how to pray. Prayer should come from you, the man. It's okay if you are not religious, but you need to know religion. We are trying to save a generation of weak men and the only way to begin to save them is to pray.

We need prayer to help us make wiser decisions; we need prayer to keep our sons away from harm and violence; we need prayer to keep them out of jail. Strong men pray. They are strong because they understand that God (or whomever your Savior is that you claim) created us to be the leaders on the planet. Having a connection with our Creator gives us the power and wisdom to be successful while we are alive and will give us peace when faced with death. If we want to save our sons from drugs, and gang violence we need to teach them that they are strong warriors when they pray. Men if you are not praying in front of your sons at the head of dinner tables, then you are not building your sons up for life success. In fact, you will be setting them up for imminent failure.

Men, it is utterly important that you are prayer warriors for your families and in front of your lady. Women see strength in prayerful men. When you have prayer in your life you appear confident, you appear strong, you appear humble, and you appear as the Head. Men, it does not matter if you are incarcerated, on probation, on drugs, have a drinking problem, or are in abused relationships--prayer will help you to deal with these issues. The real answer is to pray with other men. Praying in a group or with a group will help us to become great prayer warriors.

Teach Our Boys To Protect Themselves

Boys are strong and playful. As males we have testosterone that gives us an edge of violence and fuels our protective side. I believe that as men we should show our boys how to fight and protect themselves. I'm not saying that you make them violent to bully kids, but you have to show them how to defend themselves because it gives them a sense of self-reliance, independence and self- esteem. Whether it is boxing, martial arts, etc., you need to teach a boy how to fight.

I also believe that at the appropriate age you need to teach a boy how to handle a weapon, whether it is a BB gun, air rifle, cross bow, handgun, or hunting rifle. I also believe that you should show boys how to protect their mothers, sisters, and other family members.

Men it's these things that enable our boys to identify who they are and who they are to be as young men. When you empower them to protect themselves and teach them responsibility then they develop as strong men.

Teach Young Men How To Think And Reason

Men and boys think differently than women and girls. Boys think in simple ordered, one—two---three instructions, whereas girls think in totality. Boys focus on one task at a time, whereas girls multitask on many different things. Boys think logically before emotionally, and girls think emotionally before logically. When you understand how boys thinks differently from girls you can better relate and communicate with them.

As a man when you teach a boy how to think you need to do this by having him accomplish certain tasks. By doing tasks it enables him to think in orderly steps and by following instructions. When a boy does things repetitiously he will begin reasoning out patterns. When he starts to think in patterns then he will figure out different problems systematically.

Boys think and reason well when there are clear rules and boundaries. This is why when you are raising a boy it is helpful to define what their boundaries are. Boys learn who they are by pushing these boundaries. A father's responsibility is to help them understand why they cross these boundaries and how to successfully grow these boundaries.

An example is going from riding a bicycle to getting his learner's permit and teaching him to drive. The father's role is to teach him about cars, the responsibility of maintaining a car, teaching him how to drive, and how to respect the rules of the road to be a good driver.

You teach a boy to become a man through a series of steps and tasks. This is why coaching is a great profession to teach men how to develop. Chess is also a perfect sport to teach a young man how to think and reason. Chess requires thinking out steps to achieve a goal in a systematic and logical fashion. It takes thinking and reasoning up to 5 to 7 steps ahead in order to win the game. I advise fathers and sons to take up chess as a great teaching sport for both of you because to a man, life is a chess game.

Teach Young Men How To Build Friendships And Networks

As men we all have friends, but it's the quality of friends that will determine how successful we will become. Men fall into two categories in life and some evolve from one category to another. These categories are leaders and followers. Some boys are great leaders because they were good followers, some boys will always be followers but with the right influences in their life they can become great leaders.

As responsible leaders in the world men need to teach boys and young men how to build good reliable friendships. Men need to teach their sons how to pick friends with integrity and need to make sure that they have integrity with their friends. Men need to teach boys how to resolve conflicts by talking, sometimes it may be by fighting it out, but as long as they resolve their issues as young men and learn to bury the hatchet, then things will be okay.

All boys evolve in their friendships; boys that were friends in 3rd grade may not be friends in 6th grade. This is okay, the main point is that you make sure that your sons are growing and evolving in their friendships. This also means that as a father you need to try and have a stable home environment for your children so that they can have meaningful friendships with their friends. To have good friendships growing up means they will be well adjusted and become a productive citizen in society. In other words, make sure your sons are not building friendships with bad kids or potential criminals.

Building a network is something that comes as a young man develops into a grown man. I don't just mean Facebook networks either. I mean professional and social networks with common interests. It's important to teach young men to have networks of associates. This may include fraternities, volunteer groups, civic organizations or business organizations. It's very important that young men build networks to become successful in life. Networks help us as men to get into leadership positions and this is ultimately what all men are aspiring to grow to.

If you are a young man then you need to find an organization to become a part of to help grow you into a successful man, and if you are a father, mentor, or family member then you need to make sure the young men around you are connected to a positive network.

4TH LESSON: HOW REAL MEN BUILD SOLID & COMMITTED RELATIONSHIPS

Okay my brothers, we are going to discuss the world of relationships. There are a lot of areas to discuss here. We will cover the issues that men face in building and keeping relationships. I'm also going to talk about men's secret desires and what they may want and need in a relationship.

What Men Want In Women

Now I can't answer for every man but what I think men want is: excitement, honesty, fun, sexy, smart, tall, short, thick, thin, dark, light, short hair, long hair, black, white, Italian, Asian. Men desire all sorts of women. We all have different preferences and different tastes in women. For some men we are open to all types, and some men are very specific. Men this is normal to like and date many types of different women so you can find out what you like as a preference.

The main point here is to find out what you like about a woman and make a mental note when it is time to find the right woman for you. Remember dating is what I call "Discovery". It is to discover what you like so you can be real with yourself and find what you need to make you happy in a long lasting relationship.

Are You Ready To Be COMMITTED?

Wow, the "C" word! What exactly does this mean?

Well men, society implies that to be committed means that you are locked down to one woman for the rest of your life and that you cannot live and be who you are. This is not what being committed is about.

Now being in a committed relationship *does* mean that you make a decision to love one person at a time. Now, I must say that in other cultures a male may have more than one committed partner in a relationship. No matter what your family background is you need to understand who you love and how important they are to you and follow your societal or family values on building a committed relationship.

Men it takes a great maturity to be in a committed relationship. Some men believe we are designed by nature to procreate with numerous women. This is part of the reason why monogamy is somewhat of a struggle for many men around the globe. But, does this mean we cannot be in a monogamous and committed relationship? Of course not my brothers--this just means that you will need to work at being a bit more mature and disciplined in decisions when focusing on a committed relationship.

So let's dig a bit deeper. What is committed really?

Men it means dating a woman for a while until you feel that you only want to be with her and only her. It means that you feel that you only want to focus on that person and you feel that you don't want that person to focus on anyone but you. Now men commitment is hard and dedicated work. There is no need to sugar coat this, this is why I'm being blunt here and telling you if there is any doubt that you do not want to just be with one woman or that you don't want to focus your time and energy on just one person--then DO NOT enter into a committed relationship.

Being in a committed relationship is a man's leadership position.

Never let a woman decide *for* you that it's time to be in a committed relationship. She may want that from you, but never get into a situation of commitment because you are pressured or manipulated, or just because she is pregnant. A commitment should always be formed on a foundation of love and nothing else. Obligation is never a reason to be in a committed relationship. In the next section my brothers, we will be talking about the real work in building a committed relationship and see if this is something that each of you are ready for.

An Enlistment Of Commitment

My brothers I'm not sure if any of you have ever been in the military, or worked on contract work, or started your own business. The point I'm trying to get to is that in all of these areas there is a commitment to the task. In the military--which is the most direct commitment--you are dedicated to your country, your comrades, and the mission. Starting your own business involves being committed to creating the business, opening, operating, and being dedicated to making it succeed. These commitments take years of dedication.

When you are committed to the mission at hand men, you have to learn to be focused and do what it takes to stay committed and do a great job. Sometimes my brothers, there are times that we do things that we do not always *want* to do but for the greater good of the relationship we do what we *need* to do. Men, it's this sort of dedication and work that is needed for a good committed relationship.

Real Men Start Good Committed Relationships

Now let's assume you have been dating one or two nice women that you have been seeing for a while and you are ready to lock one woman down. Men, I respect that you are honest with yourself and you allow yourself to date, or "mess with" as we like to say, a couple women.

The reason I say that is because too often we are not allowing ourselves to adequately explore our options and we move to quickly into relationships we are not happy in. But, at the same token if you are dating more than one woman then understand that real men communicate this to the women they are dating and let them know that you are involved with more than one person.

Now, I know this may sound ludicrous, but trust me on this one men, it eliminates a lot of undue drama and heartache if you just let the women know that you are just dating and you are not ready to be in a committed relationship. It's not just about honesty and integrity men, it's about being a leader at all times and about you dictating when you are ready to be in a committed relationship. Remember women follow our lead and if she does not understand that you are in dating mode and not commitment mode then perhaps you need to communicate that more directly, or you need to find another option.

So, you have been hopefully dating a nice lady for a couple of months and you have made a decision that you would like to be in a committed relationship with her. Hopefully, you both have had a good dating history over the last couple of months and you wish to take this dating relationship to the next level. At this point as the leader in the relationship I recommend that you make this a big event.

Take her to dinner and ask her like you would in a marriage proposal. Tell her "I've really enjoyed our time dating and I was thinking that I would like to take this to the next level and have a committed relationship with you". Now you ask her "do you feel the same about our relationship and are you ready to be in a committed relationship with me at this time?" Whatever her answer make sure you listen and respect it. Men in some instances she may like you but may not be ready. For others, she will hopefully say yes.

When she says "yes" this is the time that you will want to discuss what a committed relationship means to both of you. Does it mean we can have opposite sex friends? Does it mean that you cannot have any other women's numbers in your phone? Does this mean that you have to give up some of your friends?

Make sure you discuss this fully because this is where the commitment starts and must be clearly defined, and you will start to really see what type of woman you have. Now men, once you hash out the rules of the relationship you have to be focused and committed to adhering to these rules. If you find a conflict inside this relationship this is where COMMUNICATION plays a major and crucial role.

Men You Need To Communicate In A Relationship

Okay my brothers this is an area that is lacking with so many of us. The problem that we keep falling into and tearing up our relationships and marriages is the lack of communication. For some reason we have been taught by example when growing up that we should hold things in as a way to deal with them. We feel that real men do not discuss their feelings, or we do not show a weak or vulnerable side. Men again this is BULLCRAP!

Real men COMMUNICATE, and we should do it loudly and boldly. Again, we are leaders and leaders speak up. This does not mean yelling and screaming men. This does not mean sarcastic, immature, smart-ass answers. This also does not mean talking down to your mate or demeaning them or damaging their self-esteem. If you are doing any of these things then you are communicating improperly and you are not being a real man here.

Real communication starts with listening. You must slow your minds down and start to listen to your mate or your spouse. Listen men, listen, listen, listen! Dammit LISTEN! Okay did you hear that?

Now when you listen, DON'T INTERRUPT!

I said don't interrupt whomever you are speaking to. When you interrupt the conversation and do not allow the other person to speak this means you are immature, remedial and simple. I'm just saying men, it is what it is. Let's be in control here and handle the situation. Again we are leaders. So when you are communicating listen first, and *then* respond.

When you speak men keep an even tone and keep your response to the subject at hand. Don't bring up things that have nothing to do with the problem or subject you are discussing. When you are not staying on point with the issue you are discussing you again appear immature and unintelligent. Men as true leaders you cannot be immature or unintelligent in your communications. The goal is always to speak in wisdom and not speak as if you lost your minds.

Communication comes in different forms. There is nonverbal (without words) and verbal (with words). Men, you have to be aware that your appearance, the way you stand, cross your arms, or how you walk up to someone and stand in their personal space all make up your nonverbal communication.

Men it is so important that you are aware how you appear nonverbally to your mate. Are you aggressive and intimidating when you approach her and speak to her, or are you non-threatening and passive? There is a fine line here that I want each of you to master and that is your nonverbal communication.

When you approach your mate you should always appear tall, strong and upright--never slouching, small and timid. Always try and keep a non-threatening posture, and try not to cross your arms when you are communicating. Keep your hands out of your pockets, and don't play with your hands and fingers--this shows nervousness and uncertainty.

As men you always want to have a posture of confidence, security, and leadership. The way you appear to your mate will surely reflect how she will respect you and your words. You always want your mate to be receptive to your communication, never intimidating or weak. So keep a strong posture at all times when you communicate to anyone, especially your mate.

Now let's talk about the verbal communication. Words mean POWER! Kings, leaders, and conquerors use words to build and create. They should never be used to DESTROY anyone or anything. Please understand men that your words have created countries, businesses, and even life.

Just as much as your words can build up people, they could destroy people and make them even want to commit suicide. You as men are responsible for your words. You cannot say things that are mean, degrading, and stupid. You cannot say things to loved ones that you do not mean--this is ignorant.

Real men listen and think carefully about what they say. This is why the President is such a good communicator. He carefully plans what he says before the American people so that when he speaks as their leader people will listen and respond. When you speak you need to act as if you are the President. Remember that if you speak intelligently then people will listen to you just like the President.

You need to learn to be straight-forward, honest, and real when you speak to your mate. Stop the game-playing, the lying, and hiding facts, always talk real and straight from the hip.

As men we are strong by our words and we are defined by what we say and how we say it. When speaking you should always speak clearly, loudly, and distinctly. No man should mumble his words, or whisper his words. A man should say things with authority.

Mean what you say. If you say it then you own it. In other words, remember you are always responsible for what you say. Never be put in a position to lie about what you say. Never put yourself in a position as a man where people question the honesty of your words. From time to time on television, on interviews, politics, etc. there seem to be men that back pedal or try to retract what they say. And time and time again I see the media discredit them as men because they did not own up to what they said. I have more respect for a man that stands up and admits he said something even if it was wrong, versus a man that attempts to run from his own words. This is clearly acting like a weak punk. We are here to be men not punks.

As men, when you communicate you should listen and then respond with intelligence and control. Don't ever say things you do not mean, and whatever you say, say it strong and boldly. And always, always own up to what you say.

Men Keep It Real In A Relationship

This is where we will talk about maneuvering through a relationship. To keep a good relationship going it takes a combination of communication, interaction, and compromise. If you fail to do any of these things then I assure you that if your relationship fails it will surely be because of one of those areas.

We've already talked about communication--you have to talk and share ideas in a good relationship. If you don't enjoy talking then a relationship will be very hard to maintain.

But communication is not enough by itself. To have a successful relationship, men, you have to have interaction. This involves doing activities together, spending quality time with each other, touching and kissing, and yes, sex. This is a crucial area that helps to bond and grow a relationship. This is often why I think long distance relationships are very hard for us men to maintain and thus I try to not recommend doing it, but it most certainly can be done with focus and dedication on both parts.

The last important element needed to insure a successful relationship is compromise. Being a great leader in a relationship means being able to work well with your mate and learning to be a great compromiser. Compromise means hearing your mate and getting their opinion on things and as a leader taking their opinion or viewpoint into consideration when making decisions.

A relationship takes two and it takes the minds and hearts of two people to be successful. If you or your mate are not willing to compromise on things then you definitely will not have a successful relationship. A relationship should be a positive and growing partnership where both individuals work for the good of the relationship. Men, if you think it's only your way or the highway, I can guarantee you will not be in a relationship long. If you want to be the only boss and you only want a partner who follows everything you say, this is possible, but only in certain cultures and with certain partners, so I encourage you that if this is the type of partner you wish to have then you should seek this type of mate.

There are women who are traditional and want a true leader who also believe that whatever the man says goes. Men, it is okay to want that type of partner, just be honest with yourself about what type of mate you want and seek that so you can be truly happy.

Keeping it real in a relationship means verbalizing at all times what you want and need out of the relationship. It is never the time to get into a commitment and then sacrifice your happiness. A relationship is a partnership where both parties can experience happiness. If you are not happy then you should not be in the relationship. The relationship is and will be the foundation for a possible marriage so this definitely is not the time to compromise your wants and needs.

Men, a successful relationship is to provide you with everything that you want, not sacrifice who you are. So with that said, be clear and bold about the things that you want in your relationship. Once you communicate that clearly then give your mate an opportunity to fulfill those needs and wants. But also, make sure that if she has needs and wants that you are clearly working hard to fulfill them also. If you find that you cannot fulfill those requests then make sure that you keep it real and let your mate know, or you may have to make a decision that this is not the relationship for you.

My brothers, the best type of a relationship is one with understanding and maturity. Being jealous and insecure is weak. Being possessive is weak. Real men are secure in who they are and confident in a relationship. I assure you men there are millions of women in the world that will appreciate you and treat you like the King you are supposed to be.

You should NEVER just settle for a woman just because she looks attractive, or has money, or has an education. Kings, leaders, and conquerors DO NOT SETTLE! We choose, we decide, we dominate. Men it is so important that you know who you are and who you are created to be. Again, you are the leader in a relationship, you are!

Real Men Are Not Possessive Or Insecure

I never can understand these men that must be extremely possessive over another human being. We don't own people, and we don't own women. You should be confident as a man that if you are a good man then that woman will be with you voluntarily.

For all of you insecure men that think your woman wants every other man when you are out, or if she is out on her own you are right! As long as you continue to act that way, in the back of her mind she will want another man that is not possessive and insecure.

Insecurity is not a good thing. It means you lack self-confidence somewhere and believe me when you are insecure other men see it and they see your insecurities with your woman. You need to understand that when you are possessive this is not a sign of strength it is a sign of weakness. As a man when I see a man overly possessive with his lady it immediately tells me he is insecure with something and that his woman knows he is insecure as well.

Jealousy is another sign of insecurity. You can be a little jealous, but believe me fellas, it is not attractive in the long run. It takes maturity and understanding not to be jealous, and a good woman will not want to be around a man who is constantly jealous all the time. Excessive jealousy means that you cannot have good interactions. Eventually she will leave the relationship due to your constant insecurities.

As men I need you to understand that we always need to be confident in ourselves. Another common problem is that women may view us as weak because of our insecurities in a relationship. We need to know that the woman that chooses to be in a relationship with us loves and respects us for who we are. Women decide to be in a relationship with us because they like us for us, and they love us because we make them happy. That's it men. Simple, plain-spoken and straight to the point---there is no complicated answer. So be confident that she is with us because a woman's heart belongs to us and they are designed to love willingly and freely.

Confidence Is Sexy Men

Women find confident men sexy. It doesn't matter if you are a slim 5'2", 135lbs or a big man at 6'8", 355lbs. As long as you are confident then a woman will find you highly attractive. When you are in a relationship being a confident man is very important. Women base their security off of your confidence.

Here is a secret--the more confident you are about the relationship, the more confident and secure your mate will feel about the relationship. As I stated earlier you are the leader of the relationship, and women are designed to follow your lead. When you speak to your mate, speak with confidence and assurance. When you make decisions do it with confidence. When you are out in public with her always appear confident and strong. Men always try to walk, talk, and have an attitude of confidence.

Men Hold Your Tempers

I know we have all kinds of strong men in the world, and with that being said with strong men come strong characters. Men, it's crucial that you understand that your temper is the emotional connection that you have with your inner manhood. We all have a temper. Whether you are mild-mannered or a hot head, we all have the ability to have tempers.

The thing to remember the most is that as a man you need to CONTROL your tempers. Losing your cool and letting your temper out is okay when you are provoked or attacked, but is not cool in an argument. Losing control is not what leaders do. When you are with your mate it's utterly important that you try to never lose your temper. Can you guarantee that you won't lose it? You can never guarantee that but you can at least try. When someone makes you lose your temper you allow them to take control of your emotions. Men you should never lose your temper. As a leader you need to always focus on keeping a cool and level head. Keeping a cool head allows you to always make clear and responsible decisions and a leader always needs to make clear decisions.

Real Men Allow Themselves To Love

This is the area that I find thousands of men trying to deal with around the world. Men you are allowed to love. I give you permission to love your girlfriend, your wife, your friend, your father, your mother, and your children. There are men everywhere who have issues with love and being able to allow themselves to trust and love someone.

Men, we were designed to love and protect those closest to us. If you have trouble loving in a relationship then this is an area of concern that you will want to address. Men are *made* to love--this is God's wish for us. We were made to be strong and to love and to populate the world and share HIS love. This is originally why man was made. Men were made to spread the Word of God and protect His message.

Men I give you permission to love because you were created and allowed to love. So do not be fearful to love who you are willing to open your heart to. Do not be afraid to get hurt also, because the bottom line is that you will never experience true love if you are afraid to get hurt. Love is a wonderful risk and men are risk takers.

Are YOU Ready To Get Married?

Here it is my Kings, my leaders, my conquerors--we are going to talk about knowing when you are ready to get married. First, I like to tell men that wherever you are in your dating relationship, when you get married it is like freezing the relationship then intensifying it times ten. In other words, if things are going good then it will be great when you get married, if things are shaky or there are major problems, then things will quickly get worse when you get married. We have too many divorces as it is and I'm not about to set you up for failure men. It is too important to get your foundation in order before you decide to get married.

Getting married involves making a patient, wise, and emotional decision. This is not one that should be rushed or pressured.

Remember you are always the leader of the relationship. You should also remember you do not get married out of obligation or as a favor. Marriage is the incredible institution of God's love and favor on each of us. This means that marriage should have the utmost respect and honor. Men, marriage is very, very serious. Marriage takes understanding, patience, and maturity. If you do not have these things then marriage will not be a good choice for you. Love is the reason to get married, but you should know deep in your heart that you should feel as if you could not live without her. When you reach this point and you feel that she is in the same place as you are after communicating with each other, then this a good time to discuss marriage.

I still believe in the old fashioned way of asking your bride's father (if he is alive and an active part of her life) for permission to have her hand in marriage. If he is not alive, or involved in her life then asking her mother or brother for permission is good. The reason we do this men is to establish a good relationship with her family, to show them you are a REAL MAN, and to work out any problems that you may have with them. Men, doing this takes leadership and responsibility. If you truly love her and you are ready to take care of her, then speaking to her family is a great way to start the marriage.

My brothers, I always believe it is great to discuss getting married with a close friend, preferably your father, brother, or a mentor whose opinion really matters. I think that men should get wise counsel and insight if you are truly ready on all fronts to get married. Who best can tell you the truth but someone who really knows you inside and out? I know many of you say "well I am a man and I know when I am ready to get married". Well, I'm here to tell you that if you ask some of your older and more experienced men, they would advise you that it would have been great to have spoken to someone about getting married before they did. Reason being, it might have guided some of them to really think about it before they made that final decision and it may have helped them in their marriages and to even avoid divorce.

Men divorce is ugly, tiring, and it tears down thousands of men daily, monthly, and yearly. We want to make good decisions from the beginning so we do not pay for them dearly with custody battles, child support, and loss of property and dignity later on.

Men, this is a hard statement for some of you to accept, but I'm going to say it and then I want you to think about it and discuss it with your mentors and your friends.

I believe men should wait until age 30 to get married.

Now, let me explain why I say this. First, I have observed hundreds of men, some in successful marriages and some in numerous divorces. I've realized that our "Love Maturity" is not fully developed until we at least reach age 30. I'm not saying that we as men are not mature, or not as mature as women. What I am saying is that I believe that men do not fully understand love, dating, and commitment beginning until at least the age of 30. I hear so many men say they did not date long enough, or they married too young, or they did not really know what love was. This is common and normal.

I'm here to tell you that it is okay to wait until at least between the ages 30 to 35 to be married. Now it is your prerogative to get married before age 30 but I highly advise against it. I also do not believe a man truly knows his inner manhood until age 30 or beyond. Just as boys must have time to develop, we as men need time to grow internally in our hearts and understand our King roles. If you do not feel certain about marriage then it is clearly not the time to get married.

Men, let me confirm this fact for you. WHEN YOU ARE 100% CONFIDENT IN GETTING MARRIED AND YOU ARE NOT SCARED OR DOUBTFUL, ONLY THEN ARE YOU READY.

Finances Are Crucial In Marriage

Finances are necessary for a marriage. If no one has taught you about this area of marriage then this is exactly why you have this book to guide you.

The key point here is that you are a "PROVIDER". You are the leader of this relationship. To provide for a new marriage you must have adequate employment. This is a requirement for a man. If you do not have a job then you have no business getting married. If you need two part-time jobs then you do it if you wish to be married. Our ability to provide for our household is directly tied to our manhood. I assure you if you cannot provide you are setting yourself up for your woman to disrespect you and her family to lose respect for you.

Now it does not mean that you will always make more than she does. We live in a world now where a woman can make more than her counterpart. This is okay, but you need to know that you ALWAYS want to work toward improving your financial situation. This may mean to further your education, or improve your work skills, or change industries. Whatever the decision, a King must run his kingdom. A leader must lead--that is our role. If you want to get married then make sure you have a solid and well thought out plan of how you will provide. If you are not ready to be a provider then you are clearly not ready to be married.

Men, work on improving your credit. A crucial part of improving your finances and being a provider is that the man has good credit. Men, I am here to teach you that you must be responsible as leaders to get your credit in order now! It starts with getting your income in order and then you can focus on your credit. It all works systematically. When you have good income coming in then you can fix your credit if it is not in good standing.

Additionally, you will not have to use credit if you are responsible. Every man should go online and review his credit history every year on your birthday. This is how I remember to do it. Be sure to review reports from the 3 credit bureaus: Transunion, Equifax, and Experian. When reviewing these reports, make sure your information is correct and that you do not have outstanding past due balances that can negatively affect your credit rating.

If you do, then take into consideration your income and develop a plan that allows you to work diligently and intelligently to pay these things off. You can contact each creditor and offer a settlement or payment plan. This should be your priority before you get married or it should be a priority while you are married.

A FICO credit score range will be anywhere between 300 to 800. Your goal should be to get to 680 or better. This is done by paying all of your obligations on time or early, and making sure you don't have past due balances. Also, you should have no more than two major credit cards. All others should be eliminated and paid off. After your credit is on the road to recovery, the next step is to have a savings account. This savings account is a separate account and you should have a goal to save at least $1000 to begin with and then work it up to $5,000, then $10,000. This will not happen overnight gentlemen but remember this is the foundation to being a good provider.

Good providers think about their family first and their wants second. Men, if you begin to think this way you will be on a great road to securing the finances in your marriage. You must also make sure that your spouse is responsible and knowledgeable about her credit and finances because each partner's finances affects the other's. Make sure you both are honest and have a detailed discussion of where your finances are as a couple before and after you get married, and make sure you both believe in the same ways as to how to handle finances. If not, then you will surely have financial problems in the marriage which will certainly lead to divorce. Remember you are both supposed to be partners in this. I recommend that you read Dave Ramsey's book. "***Total Money Makeover***". It is the bible to financial stability for a great marriage. Get it and study it my brothers.

Separate Or Joint Accounts

My brothers I have been asked this hundreds of times. Should you have a separate checking account or joint account? I believe this is a matter of preference. I do believe if you are NOT married you should maintain separate accounts, even if you are living together. When you get married I believe it is okay to still have separate accounts as well as a joint account to share finances. But, when you are married, if you decide to only have one joint account this is perfectly fine as well.

Men this is why your finances and your credit should be in order. A man should be in control of his finances at all times. Make sure you are responsible with your accounts and try not to over draw them.

Pre-Marital Counseling and Marriage Counseling for Men

My brothers, I believe pre-marital counseling is extremely important nowadays before one decides to get married. All leaders seek wise counsel or have a team to mentor and guide them through important life decisions. There is absolutely nothing wrong with having pre-marital counseling to make sure that certain things are pointed out to you and to have clarity before making a major life decision. I advise all men to have pre-marital counseling to confirm that all issues and concerns are brought to the table up front.

Now let's talk about while you are in your marriage. No matter if you are married for a month or 50 years, marriage counseling is a wise tool to use if you are having problems in your marriage. Marriage counseling does a few things to repair whatever is wrong. First, it gives you a third party who is unbiased to analyze your situation and who can listen without an agenda. Secondly, it will allow you to speak freely and provide some understanding to your mate on how you feel and what you are going through. Lastly, it will show your mate that you sincerely care about saving the relationship.

Men, strong and real men who love and care to try and save their family look at marriage counseling as a productive tool. So all of you that say "no man can tell me how to love my wife or tell me how I should act" are being horrendously ignorant and you will definitely lose your wife and family if you are not open to counseling. Remember, great leaders are open to wise counsel. If you are close-minded then you are definitely setup for failure in your marriage. If you could have fixed the problems yourself they would have been fixed!

Real men submit themselves humbly and seek wiser counsel. If you are rejecting marriage counseling while your spouse is begging for it then take this as a clear sign that she feels there is a chance to save the marriage. Do not let your anger, your temper, and narrow mindedness blind you from saving your marriages.

Again you are the leaders of the relationship and of the household. Everything is your responsibility and the success of the marriage is your responsibility. Once you own that responsibility it is your goal to use all of the resources available to you to complete the mission of saving the relationship. Please my brothers do not wait until it is too late to get marriage counseling. It does not matter who you talk to. It could be your pastor at the church or a trusted friend, but I always recommend a professional that deals with this on a regular basis.

And men remain dedicated to the process and see it through all the way to the end. You must also participate and apply what you are learning about each other and the solutions that are presented to bring you back together. Men please understand that going to marriage counseling will not guarantee success or always solve the problems, but you as a leader must try and try with all of your might to work through the issues and apply different solutions. Real men go to marriage counseling!

Why Do Men Cheat?

Okay my brothers I'm not here to psychoanalyze men in this section. And I'm not here to solve any problems here about why men cheat. What I am here to do is have a discussion on what we as men go through, and help you to understand it so at the end of this ride we can make better choices for our relationships and marriages. So let's get on this rollercoaster.

Men, there are mainly two reasons why people cheat. People cheat because of a lack which creates a need or because of a want. Let's break this down. Before we go any further, we have to determine what exactly is considered cheating to society and our mates. Men, to cheat as it is defined is to violate a committed relationship. Cheating may be going to lunch or dinner with a female you are interested in while you are in a committed relationship.

Cheating may be texting another female while in a committed relationship and the text contains words that are beyond just friendship. Cheating may be that you are watching pornography without the knowledge of your mate. Men as crazy as this all sounds these are some of the things that our mates and spouses consider cheating in a committed relationship. The thing here is that we understand that all men are susceptible to crossing the fine lines of cheating. The question here that I wish to present is do you understand the boundaries of cheating so that you do not cross them in a committed relationship? If not, it's okay. We will work through this each step of the way.

Men, cheating is not a sickness, or a condition that we must take medication to cure. It is a decision, a matter of discipline and a reflection of how much value we place on a particular relationship that helps us to stay focused and dedicated. Discipline must be joined hand in hand with maturity, this is why I stress considering marriage after age 30. When we are mature then we can truly understand the value of a relationship. But again, with this in mind it does not mean we do not cheat. Instead it just helps us to hopefully make better decisions about our wants and desires so that we don't have to cheat.

To work on reducing or eliminating cheating altogether it first starts with being brutally honest with yourself my brothers. If you want a woman with long hair, or a big butt, or big breasts, or she needs to be mixed, or white, or black then you must be brutally honest with yourself. If you want a woman who is brilliant, or funny, or just a party girl then again you must be brutally honest with yourself. If you are an affectionate man and your mate is not then you must be brutally honest about your needs. If your spouse does not want to perform oral sex, or do some sexual things you desire then you must be honest with yourself. From this point you need to determine if you are happy with what you have and work at compromising and fixing these things in the relationship, or you may need to make a tough decision to leave the relationship. Either way, we cheat because we lack having our needs fulfilled or do not get the things that we desire or want.

Again, we as men are leaders in our relationship and I'm praying that by speaking with you that we can take our leadership, mix it with integrity and build upon that to be more committed and focused in our relationships and marriages. I want to give you whatever I can as a fellow man and mentor to help to eliminate the drama that comes with cheating. I don't want to see any of you on the show "Cheaters", where we are constantly degrading our manhood with footage of our indiscretions.

We are meant to be kings and leaders, not shameful, minute men that are known to be incredibly unfaithful and untrustworthy. This is not who we are as men, this is not who YOU are meant to be or are defined as being. Men, we must work harder at becoming more committed and focused on our happiness and the happiness of our spouses.

All I am here to tell you is that you must be honest in defining what you want and stick to it. If you can communicate your wants and desires to your mates or your wives then do it and truly work at eliminating the outside distractions like other women and focus on fixing your relationship. This is only if **YOU WANT TO**. But it can only work when you make the decision to be disciplined and focused. If you decide not to, then I tell you that you have permission to walk away from the relationship if that is not where you desire to be. A real man will not hold his mate hostage in a relationship that is not fulfilling to both parties. The real integrity is to let go of the relationship and pursue what you truly need and what you truly want.

Men if you truly want to find resolution for your cheating there is help to assist you in that process. I recommend first making a decision as to whether you want to be committed or you want to be free. Next, you need to work at eliminating your outside distractions. This means getting rid of and deleting old phone numbers, and ending all outside relationships. Next, if you need outside help then I recommend that you find a counselor or some sort of support group to help you and your spouse work through the issues. If they cannot be worked out then understand that this should be a development period, and just know that you may need to grow and move on from your relationship.

Men I pray that if you are in a relationship where cheating is involved that you find your way out of it and save your efforts to devote to finding and cultivating the relationship that you desire to be in.

Relationships And Marriages Are Real Work

My brothers, relationships and marriages are hard work. Being committed to something is already hard work, plus add to it working to keep your mate happy and that equals *very* hard work. Again, I'm not here to make this seem like it's cookies and cream to keep a good relationship together. I need all of you to understand that marriage is discipline.

Just because something looks nicer across the street does not mean we can just run and get it. You will and have to say no to temptations that threaten your relationship. Avoiding temptations is really hard work. But it must be done if you wish to have a good and committed relationship.

Men, I'm telling you that keeping a very low number of female friends and acquaintances will help you make the job of a relationship much easier. Maintaining relationships with friends that encourage you to be faithful to your mate also helps. Those friends that have you hanging out in the bars and strip clubs late at night are not good influences on a good relationship. Real men know what to do to keep their home life happy.

Trust me gentlemen, the same friends that have you partying late in the clubs may be the same friends that will talk to your woman when you break up with her. Stay dedicated men and be real men and honor and fight for your relationships.

5TH LESSON: REAL MEN & TABOO ISSUES

My brothers, if there is anything that I have tried to accomplish with this book it is to make sure that I keep it real as possible and be able to discuss real issues that men go through every day, every month, and every year. In the next few sections we will talk about the taboo things that are very difficult for many men to deal with.

So let's talk.

Real Men Have Been Abused

There have been over 5 million men that have been abused in some form or another growing up, and those are the just some of cases that actually have been reported over the last 15 years or so. This abuse can be sexual or physical. Cases of abuse to young boys and teenage boys are real and we have to acknowledge this epidemic that hurts our young men.

Young boys that have been abused go through a myriad of issues that affect them incredibly later in life. Abuse impairs a man's ability to build good trusting relationships, it hinders us from engaging in good communication with others, and it prevents us from developing good, healthy and loving intimate relationships.

If you are a boy or man that has been abused in some way, I

want to reach out to you and let you know that you are no less of a man. If anything, you are a real man for enduring such a tragedy in your life. I do know that you may feel that most people will never understand the hurt and pain that you went through in your childhood, but I can tell you that there are many, many, many men that are dealing with it daily. What I can also tell you is that there is help and assistance in this area and I encourage you to seek out this help from a religious leader, a counselor, or a peer group.

As a man we all pray to have our lives in order. I can say that God does not dislike you, nor is He mad at you. What I have learned is that God is a Father who only loves us and wants us to live life abundantly and successfully. What I also know is that there is evil in the world and that the devil seeks to destroy good men because we are the leaders of the world. Without evil we would not know good nor would we know that we can and should turn to our Heavenly Father for healing and strength. I pray that all of my young boys and men that were abused are healed and are able to have a more productive life and may have more fulfilling and loving intimate relationships. For my men that physically or sexually abuse young men, I pray that you seek help immediately to get a grip on this problem. I also pray that if you continue in this behavior that God removes you from this earth before a real man figures you out and decides to do so.

Men That Abuse Women

Now this is an important section. I must say that I do not understand boys or men that abuse or hit women. Abuse of women can consist of mental abuse or physical abuse or both. I cannot understand why as men we feel it is okay to verbally demean and disrespect the women that are supposed to respect us and honor us as leaders and protectors.

Men, I have no respect for men that abuse women. Now I do know that we are influenced by the "old school" mentality of some men to intimidate and scare our women to "keep them in line". But the truth is men that if you have to talk down to, demean, call a woman out of her name, disrespect, hit, and beat a woman then you are no man to me or society. This behavior is uncalled for. As real men you must understand if your woman does not respect you or give you the respect you deserve, then the problem is either you are not a real man to her, or you selected the wrong mate. Either way my brothers, abusing women only leads to one direction and that is unneeded drama and going to jail.

Again, you must remember that you are defined as a man by how well you respect others and how they respect you. When you abuse a woman you appear to be less than a man, and you are then perceived as weak, not strong. The real issue I see is that men who abuse women usually cannot stand up to a real man. These men believe it's easy to intimidate who they consider to be the weaker vessel (women) and cannot stand up to other men. If this is you then you do have a problem that must be dealt with immediately.

If you are constantly fighting with your mate and you see yourself cursing and talking down to your mate then I suggest you either leave that situation before it escalates into something that will land you in jail. If you are hitting your mate then I strongly suggest that you seek some counseling to fix this issue. It is crucial in your development as a man that you do not abuse women. This may be a sign that you have a temper and anger issues and this sort of behavior not only leads to jail but also possible homicide of your mate or for yourself if she decides one day to retaliate. Real men never abuse women.

Men That Use And Deal Drugs

Okay men, as I said, I like to keep it real at all times. I'm from Chicago and South Carolina, but no matter where I have lived or traveled I have seen that men want to be successful, rich, and will do whatever it takes to take care of their families.

Here I want to talk about our brothers that use drugs. I'm talking about everything from pain killers to heroin and cocaine. Men, when we become dependent of drugs it impairs our ability to be responsible and be the real man that God intended for us to be.

Drugs are killing our men and killing our families that must deal with our addictions. When men use drugs there is a 50% chance that our sons and daughters may also use drugs. If they do not use drugs then there is a 90% chance that it will affect our children as to the way they deal with life. Some of our children will have psychological effects of abandonment and low self-esteem. Men, make sure that if there is a problem with drugs and you need help please seek some assistance. A real man steps up and faces his issues. If you are a man and know someone that has a drug addiction then as his brother it is your duty to try and help him and save another man from destruction.

Now let me talk to my pharmaceutical entrepreneurs. The men who want to be big time drug dealers. Gentlemen, there are millions of occupations on the planet but time and time again it seems that in rough times we as men want and need to make quick money. We all have known or know someone that wants to deal in drugs. The problem here is that there is no stability in a highly illegal occupation.

Here are the issues. You are always avoiding the law. You have a high probability of making enemies that may attack you or your family at any given time. You can never trust anyone. And the life expectancy for you or your business is very limited. I do know that you can make lots of money, but men at what cost are you risking making that short-lived fortune? Also, at what cost are you willing to risk your family's safety and reputation?

I'm not here to preach to you my brothers, but what I am here to do is make you think about your options. Again we are degrading our families and our friendships by leading a life that will primarily lead to destruction. There are no successful drug dealers that made it big time without losing family or friends, or both. Every day is a risk and a balance between life and death.

Men, instead I encourage you to own a legitimate business and use your hustling talents to build an empire and a dynasty. Build something legal that your children can be proud of. Use your talents to be successful so your mates and your family can admire you with great respect. That is a true leader and what real men do.

Men, Prostitution And Pornography

Brothers, there is no need to act like we are not physical creatures by nature. As men we love the female anatomy and all of its wonderful attributes. What sort of creature would we really be if we did not admire the beauty that God has allowed us to adore and enjoy? Men, we are well aware that we love the sexiness and provocative nature of women, so there is no falsehood that as men we can become victim to it.

The thing here to know is that there are brothers that indulge in prostitution, which is the transaction of sexual favors for money or other things. What I can say is that as real men there is a fine line that we must not cross when it hurts the ones that we truly love. When you are single there is nothing wrong with wanting your sexual needs to be met, but when you are married or in a serious and committed relationship my brothers please know that if discovered that there can and will be negative consequences.

Prostitution can lead to criminal repercussions, a bad reputation, and even sexual diseases. It also can lead to dishonesty, secrets, a double lifestyle, and even blackmail and extortion. All I want to say men is that yes, you are grown and it's ultimately your life, but please be careful of the decisions you make because the price you pay can be large.

Pornography can be just as bad my brothers. The same disastrous repercussions can happen when you over indulge in porn. Now I am not saying that there is anything wrong with some types of pornography, as a matter of fact, there are some women and couples that enjoy watching pornography together.

The problem lies in when pornography is a dirty secret from your spouse or your mate. Men, there is a serious problem when you are watching or indulging in pornography that involves under-aged children. This is not appropriate, but I am aware that it goes on in the world. Men it is also not an appropriate or healthy entertainment when you spend hundreds or thousands of dollars that you cannot really afford to feed this habit. Men, do not fall into the trap of letting pornography rule your life or destroy your life. It can do just that when more than 30% of your personal or work time is involved in some sort of pornographic activity. Pornography can be an addictive behavior that has destroyed many men's lives; please don't let it rule you and keep you from being the leader you are destined to be. There are counselors and places that can help with porn addiction before it destroys your personal relationship or your family life.

Men And Gambling

My brothers, gambling is a wonderfully invigorating sport and source of entertainment but I have known a few men that have lost millions gambling. Gambling is again one of those things that can come with very serious consequences. Gambling can be addictive and can become a legitimate sickness. Do not take it lightly men.

Men are designed to be winners and be competitive, and because of that trait we can easily be pulled into a life of high rolling success, only to fall to brutal destruction in which we can lose everything. And I do mean everything--house, car, spouse, children, job, career, and even your freedom or your life. Men, gambling can literally cost you your life.

Please make sure that this is not a continuing problem for you. If you or someone you know has a gambling problem please save your brother and get some sort of intervention or counseling before he loses everything. This is what real men do for real men.

Men Dealing With Alcoholism

Brothers this is a huge problem for so many men across the globe. There are millions of men that have a problem with alcohol. When I was in the army, drinking was the rite of passage for us young men. For a lot of other young men this takes place during our college days. However you were introduced to drinking we find that many men find this as a vice or outlet that they end up using to solving or dealing with their problems. Alcoholism is a very real problem for many, many young boys and men.

Some young men start drinking in high school after they have seen their own fathers or step-fathers or even mothers drinking. Some young men even start with their friends when they go to their friend's home after school and raid their friend's parent's liquor bar. Even at some of their house parties and basement parties a lot of young people start drinking to fit in and belong with their friends. Whatever the reason that one begins drinking the fact is that if not done in moderation it can become a real and deadly problem.

Over 10 million people across the nation are dealing with alcoholism in some form or another. Either these individuals have a drinking issue or have a loved one, family member, or friend that is an alcoholic. You see it just doesn't affect the drinker, it affects those around them just as much. Family members and friends have to deal with mood swings, temper tantrums, depression, and many other signs. As fathers to our children it is so important that we work to set a positive example to them. Drinking affects our children greatly and determines how they will deal with their own problems in the future.

To all my men I encourage you that if you have a drinking issue which means that every time you drink you are getting drunk to where you don't remember what happened, this is a problem. If you are drinking daily this is a problem. If people can smell alcohol on you at your work place or out in public, men this is definitely a problem. Remember you are leaders, you are protectors, you are what women and children look up to. If you have a drinking problem men it is being a real man to get assistance to help solve this issue. I pray and encourage you men to get this taken care of for your sakes and your children's sake. Give them what they deserve and that is a sober man as their father.

Men With Post Traumatic Stress Disorder (PTSD)

My brothers, I served in Desert Storm and fought in a field artillery battalion. Not only did I see fighting but I was shot at and saw many things that people have nightmares about. PTSD is real and I'm happy that the government has accepted and realized that this is an enormous problem with our veterans, and we must recognize that it can happen with not only veterans but to anyone who has had a traumatic experience.

PTSD is a disorder that affects people when encountering stressful situations or triggers—everything from hearing loud noises to seeing violent acts. PTSD causes seizures, panic attacks, cold sweats, bad dreams, depression, and many other things. This is a definite problem that thousands of men are dealing with across the globe. War and violence are not normal practices of life and it changes us mentally. I know there are men that are very defensive in the way they act, and can be very jumpy and extremely cautious. These are all indicators that you could have mild to extreme PTSD.

For my military brothers this is a time when you should seek the help of Veterans Affairs to deal with these issues immediately. For others that have been in a traumatic experience, a robbery, a murder, a terrible accident, etc--you should seek immediate counseling to help cope with PTSD. It is real and it can hinder your growth and affect your lives and your family's lives. Men let's take care of ourselves and your fellow brothers by acknowledging and dealing with this mental issue.

Men And The Baby Momma Drama

Okay men, this goes out to all the fathers out here that are young men and for the matured grown men. We have to talk about this baby momma drama that we all have dealt with or are dealing with. So let's get started.

Men it's difficult when you have a child and you are not with the mother. God did not intend for us to be single parents to our child or children but the reality is that we are single parents or in fractured homes. Fractured homes means our child may be raised with a father and grandmother, or raised by grandparents, aunts, uncles, etc. Men, no matter what situation your children are in your kids need you as the father. Never think that your child does not want you in their lives or that they do not need you. It took two to make them and it takes two to care for them.

Please understand there are numerous reasons why baby momma drama starts. We will go over them so that you can understand where the hostility or attitudes come from. It starts when you have broken up with the mother, either because things did not work out, you cheated, she cheated, you lied, she lied, you both fight, or just because you both did not intend to have a committed relationship. Whatever the reason, the result is that you have a child or children involved in a non-committed relationship.

Men, women are emotional and they already have strong feelings that you dumped them and the child, or that you do not care about her and the child involved. This begins the negative attitude and animosity. Some women may feel like you are not a suitable father because you do not have adequate financial means, or that you are not responsible, or that you are inconsistent. Men, I really need you to look honestly at yourself and see if there is some truth to that. For some of you that is the brutal and honest truth. So be truly honest with yourself and let's begin to fix this.

Other women may feel that you put your girlfriends or other children before theirs. You must also look at this truth and see if that applies to you. If that is the truth then this is totally wrong men. Again, our children did not ask to be here on this planet. You birthed them and you are responsible for each and every child's well-being. Men, if these are accurate assessments by your child's mother then I implore you to fix these issues immediately so that she will not continue to have ammunition to keep the drama going.

The first step in limiting the baby momma drama is to first fix the issues that you have and address them immediately. Remember you are to be a provider and provide for your children. Real men take care of their seeds and their responsibilities. If you are not taking care of the child you made then this is degrading as a man.

Second, you need to have open communication and establish

boundaries with your baby momma. Communication means that you need to learn to talk to her about your child and get involved in what's happening in your child's life. This does not mean that after a conversation or two that you discuss trying to get back with her or try to have sex with her. Men, this is where the drama begins. You need to stay focused on your children first and foremost.

Establishing boundaries means that you have to limit what you say and how you say it to your child's mother. Meaning, only talk about your child or children's activities, do not talk about your personal lives, especially who you are dating or who she is dating.

Next, you should only call about your child during daytime to bedtime hours. This means if you have small children, between 8am to 8pm should be an acceptable time to speak to their mother and to speak with your child. You should try to not talk to their mother after your child goes to bed. The reason for this is that if you are dating someone then your lady will understand the proper communication etiquette and if your ex or baby momma is dating then you will not cause conflict for her and her mate.

Also men, when you talk with her about issues with your children try hard not to argue. Keep a cool and reserved tone when speaking. Try to work at having good conversations, not tense conversations that lead to arguments. Try to hear her thoughts out completely without interrupting and hopefully she will allow you to speak without interrupting you. As soon as the business with your children is concluded get off the call or end the conversation--again stay focused.

Another key factor here is to make sure that you keep your spouses or current girlfriends out of the relationship between you and your baby momma. Now your girlfriend or spouse can offer advice but communication needs to be only between you and your child's mother. Whatever opinion your mate has about your ex or child's mother, KEEP THAT TO YOURSELF. Women do not want to hear about another woman's opinion if she has nothing to do with your child. This will only make communication harder for the both of you.

Men you need to understand the rights that you have by being a father, involved or not. As a father you have the right to visitation and I encourage you to visit your child as often as agreed upon. Whether you pay child support or not, this has nothing to do with you seeing your child. The laws are clear that you have the right to see your child or children whether you are paying child support or not. And this is clear in all states.

Men your child's mother does not have the right to dictate whether you can or cannot see your child. I'm tired of seeing men intimidated by their child's mother with threats of incarceration, or of taking them to court. If you go to court men you will always be awarded visitation. Now you can work out child support, that is secondary, but the main objective is to see your child. Do not be afraid to fight for your children and work to be good fathers. It is never too late to start. Just make sure you begin working on your issues so that you can win in the end.

Men I do believe that you should do all you can within reason to see and care for your children. You should be involved and you should try to live close to your children so you can be involved in their lives. Again, they didn't ask to be here and we are all responsible men, right? Of course, we all are. We are leaders and our children are our heirs to our throne.

Baby momma drama can be minimized and even eliminated but we have to be leaders and fight for what we want and do it with a cool and level head. We cannot have tempers and anger hold us back for our child's mother to use against us, and we also cannot use underhanded means to battle them as well. Again, the only victims will end up being our children. Continue to fight to be in your child's lives.

When you begin this journey to be in their lives remember to be consistent. Be a real man, if you say you will be there for your child, then be there. If you are telling them you will call them on a certain day at a certain time then be a real man and make sure you keep that commitment. Never promise men, just tell your child you will always try your best. This way they will not be disappointed if you don't come through. But the goal is as a real man to never disappoint your children. You are there to be their hero, their Savior, everything you can to them. You have that title until you mess it up, and even then our children will forgive us time and time again because they love their father unconditionally. But try never to let that love down men.

Real men fight and die for their children. Are you willing to live for them and die for them? I hope so because if not, rest assured another real man will.

Real Men That Are Gay

So the question on this taboo issue of homosexuality is "are gay men real men"? I'm not an expert on this issue but I do feel that it is very important that we address this issue among our young and older men. I grew up in a time when gay men were viewed as "sissies" and over-the-top flamboyant, so it was not considered manly to be gay.

What I will say is that due to the violent or abusive environments that our men are being exposed too it is somewhat influencing the outcome of our men's sexual orientation. As men, we are encountering situations where our sons and other young men are becoming gay. I'm not sure if it is because of curiosity, rejection or abuse from their fathers, or the absence of their fathers. Perhaps it is just because they make the choice or they are just born gay. Either way it is a growing and apparent issue among men.

Even though a man is gay, I will say that being a man is embedded in his character. Being gay still means that a man can be a man according to common standards regarding his ability to keep his word, his bond, his loyalty, and how he respects himself and other men.

As for men that have sons and discover that their son is gay, it is crucial that we try and continue to love our sons or our brothers even though you may not agree with their orientation. It may be that loving them as men may help our sons cope with the challenges of being gay and being accepted into manhood. Being gay does not mean that we cannot love our seed and it does not mean that we cannot still teach them what men do as real men. My brothers we still need to love, encourage, and teach our young men and older men that are gay.

6TH LESSON: REAL MEN ARE SUCCESSFUL & SO ARE **YOU**

Men Are Destined To Be Successful

My brothers it is not a coincidence that we were created to lead and be successful. All of you are Kings and Warriors and were made to lead others towards success. We see this in sports teams, corporations, government, small businesses, etc. Men are strong and are risk takers by nature and it's in our DNA to be leaders.

As a man you will see challenges along your life that you will need to overcome. Just like basic training for the military these challenges are there to develop you and groom you to be a strong leader and to move you closer and closer to your life's calling. If you have had a difficult road in the past then be confident that these experiences have prepared you to get that much closer to your success.

I had the opportunity to observe the selection process for the Navy Seals and Special Forces organizations which are considered the elite of our military fighting forces. The soldiers that make the selection process go through the most grueling and difficult challenges that the human mind and body can face. All of the candidates have experienced some sort of situation that they believe prepares them for the most dangerous job on the planet.

When they go through the selection process and then the actual training after making the cut, they are then thrust into another level of excruciating challenges that seem almost unbearable to the human mind and body. The result is that the U.S. military creates the most successful fighting warriors in the world.

Again, the circumstances that we encounter are only designed to prepare us for future greatness. As men we are destined to be successful.

Men Should Be In Constant Development Mode

Brothers, we are in the process of becoming great individuals, and to become great we must develop from good to be great. If you look at some of the most talented people in their industries--Tiger Woods, LeBron James, Kobe Bryant, Denzel Washington, Tom Cruise, David Beckham, and the list goes on.

A common thread among of all these talented men is that they continuously work to become great in their talents. They work, practice, critique themselves and push themselves to be better.

To be better may mean to continue your education in your field. To be better may mean to be mentored by someone else who is an expert in that field. To be better may be to take classes, or even read a book or study a DVD to be better. Whatever your mode of learning, just learn, and make the effort to become better at your craft.

My philosophy is that you should not be the same as you were last year. Every year you should be better than the last year. Brothers, be in constant development mode. Always strive to be better the next day, and the next day.

Without A Target You Will NEVER HIT THE GOAL

Brothers what are your goals for this year? Point blank. If you do not have well thought out and written goals you will go NOWHERE!

Now don't get me wrong, you will accomplish some of your goals that you have in the back of your mind but to become better at accomplishing what you have *on* your mind you must make a mental roadmap. For the last 10 years I have been making out my list of yearly goals and the task was to work yearly at accomplishing 5 to 7 major goals for the year. On an average I would accomplish 60% to 80% of my goals—which is not a bad success rate.

Now doing this would keep me on a path to keep growing and developing. The amazing result that I realized was that if I reviewed the goal lists over the past 10 years I could track my success progression from when I wanted a new car; to building up my savings account from $100 to over $10,000; to going from getting my first apartment to owning my first home; to owning several rental properties. All of these things have been a goal at one time or another. But I had to create the plan to get there, and it all started with creating my list of goals.

Here's how we create the list.

First you need to find 5 to 7 things that you would like to accomplish just in the next 12 months. These goals need to be big, but not too big to be unrealistic, and not too small to be that simple. Also, these goals should cover the following areas: Financial, Career, Spiritual, Relationship, and Family. The following is one example of a goal list.

Shawn's Goal List 2013
1. Put an extra $3000 in my savings account
2. Purchase a new 2013 Mercedes ML 350
3. Start my new coaching business by March 31st
4. Attend Bible study every Wednesday this year
5. Work on spending more time with my girlfriend
6. Having a daddy and daughter date night every week
7. Publish my fourth book by August 1st

Now brothers this list is personal for you, but if your mate wants to share goals with you then I say this is also a way for both of you to work together, or even the whole family can create a goal list.

Now, what I do is put the list in all areas of the house where I can view it. I put it on my mirror in the bathroom, by my bed, on the refrigerator, and even on my front door when I leave daily. I even type a very small list that I can fit in my wallet or even place on the dashboard of my vehicle. The reason for this is that you must see it daily and get it in your mind to start thinking about your goals constantly. This is where your roadmap to success begins.

Now, to accompany your goal list you will need to create an "affirmation list". An "affirmation list" is a list of positive thoughts that you will need to ingrain in your mind daily to give you the fuel that you need to complete your goals. This is the "power of positive thinking" in action. As men we go through numerous struggles and road blocks through our daily lives that make accomplishing our goals difficult. Look at your affirmations as the sights on a firearm that you adjust to be able to hit your target. Or even better, look at affirmations as gas that you put into your car to drive the route to get to your goals. Affirmations are the fuel, your mind is the vehicle, and your goals are the destination. Here is an example of an "affirmation list".

Shawn's Affirmations
1. I will be a successful author and business owner
2. I am a growing student of God
3. I am a great and loving father
4. I am a great friend, spouse, and mentor
5. I will be a millionaire

Again my brothers, you can put anything you wish on this list that will motivate you and keep you focused. But, please don't think that this is not important. When it is time to make a decision or you need that encouragement to talk yourself through a tough time remembering your affirmations will get you through. Affirmations are powerful and they are crucial to your success. I can promise you that as soon as you make out these lists that your life will immediately change in a more positive and focused direction. So let's get these lists done today!

We Are Men Of Purpose And Distinction

Men, we were created for a purpose. A purpose to lead; and a purpose to make the world go round because of our protection and leadership. Men travel the globe in search of treasures, mysteries and to even find out their purpose. Distinction is the way we follow our purpose. We search for our purpose with the fierceness of a tiger but with the keenness of a fox. If we are vigilant in our search then with the grace of The Almighty we can find our purpose and live it.

We all have a purpose. Every man on the planet has a purpose for his life. The question is, what is your purpose? I can tell you what was told to me and that is that a man's purpose is to fulfill God's promise for prosperity and success through His Word. Aside from that your purpose is found inside of your talents, your skills, and your determination. How you achieve and fulfill your purpose is to do it with great distinction.

Men, when I was in the military my drill sergeants always said, ***"Private, you need to move with a PURPOSE"!*** Men, make sure you are moving through life with a purpose. If you have not realized your purpose for living then I encourage you to find your purpose quickly and live in it so you can really enjoy your life.

Real Men Mentor And Bring Up Other Men

Brothers, we have many definitions of success. Some may consider success having a big home and nice cars. Some may consider success being famous and powerful. Others may consider success having 6 or 7 figures in your bank account. All of these assessments can be correct of what success can be for you. But, what I consider success is when you take your success and bring up other men to follow in your footsteps and leave a legacy. Leaving a legacy of success means that you have to work hard to live a successful life and through your example and hard work teach another young man.

When you are able to show another man how to reach your level of success then you have reached the pinnacle of success. Showing someone else how to be successful may be done by creating a business that teaches and develops successful people. Demonstrating success can also mean taking someone under your wing and coaching them to be successful. Teaching others to reach your level of success can also mean you writing a book, sharing a blog, or creating a website that fosters success. The bottom line my brothers is that success must be shared so we all can benefit and make a better environment for success for all men.

Men Volunteer In Their Communities

When I was 32 years old my father passed away from colon cancer. It was one of the hardest times of my life. I lost my friend, my mentor, and a dad. The ironic thing that happened to me is that his passing made me take a hard look at my life and honestly think about what I have really accomplished.

What I realized is that I was just working and living an average boring life. Yes I had friends and I went out and socialized but I quickly realized that I had not done anything significant at this time. I hadn't given back to anything or anyone. This is when I decided to volunteer and give back and start living with a purpose. Brothers, I strongly encourage that you seek out ways to volunteer in your community.

Men make the world go round. I believe as the leaders of the planet volunteering exposes us to the world. Men, make sure you give back whether it's being a Boy Scout leader, a Mason, a mentor to young boys and men, a Big Brother, or just spending a little time at the YMCA. I even encourage you to establish a non-profit of some sort that gives back to the community in some way. Again, you are not truly successful until you are giving back and bringing another man up to be a success.

Men Be Real Men At ALL TIMES

My brothers it has been a journey reading and understanding this book. Every time I re-read this book it reminds me that there are men all around the world that are trying to work at being real men. The truth is all of you reading this are real men. You are a man of integrity, of honor, of respect. Being a real man means to walk with your head up high, shoulders back, speak loudly, and have self-respect. Respect yourself enough to want the best out of life. Respect yourself enough to value your freedom, and respect yourself enough to have your WORD mean what you say to anyone.

As a man make it a point to concentrate daily on working on the principles and tools in this book. Work on respecting and honoring your fellow brothers around the world, whether they are white, black, brown, green, or blue. All men are designed the same and feel the same. All men are warriors, philosophers, teachers, protectors, leaders, peacemakers, and pillars in our communities.

The decision to be a real man is yours. Do not let anyone define you, you define yourself. You can decide if you are going to be a criminal or an icon. You can decide if you are going to be a good father or a bad one. You can decide if you are going to be rich or poor, strong or weak, tell the truth or be a liar.

You decide to be a real man. Define yourself and learn to pray to be the best man that God has designed you to be.

Peace and love my brothers.

ABOUT THE AUTHOR

Shawn James has been involved in the personal development industry for over 20 years. He is a Life and Executive business coach and President of B.L. James Advisors L.L.C, an Atlanta consulting firm. He is also a public speaker, consultant, and the Chief Operations Officer of a large security company in Atlanta, Georgia.

Mr. James has worked with numerous companies and civic organizations in helping to develop and grow their influence and for the betterment of improving their communities.

Shawn's passion is to develop, mentor, and influence young people and adults around the world to find their passions, develop their dreams, and accomplish their goals and their life purpose.

Made in the USA
Coppell, TX
01 November 2020

40637627R00066